Janet Laurence began her career in advertising and public relations. In 1978, she moved to Somerset with her husband, and started Mrs Laurence's Cookery Courses, beginning with basic cookery techniques for teenagers and later introducing courses for the more advanced. She combined this with writing for the *Daily Telegraph*, eventually taking over Bon Viveur's weekly cookery column. Janet Laurence now divides her time between writing crime fiction and cookery books, and she makes regular trips to Brittany, where she and her husband have recently converted a set of ruined barns.

Janet Laurence's previous culinary whodunnits are also available from Headline, and have been widely praised:

'Exuberant tale of gastronomic homicide, full of intriguing inside-knowledge . . . Engaging chefette, Darina Lisle, sleuths zestfully and there are even some helpful culinary hints along the way' *The Times*

'Filled with mouth-watering recipes as well as mystery' *Sunday Express*

Also by Janet Laurence

FICTION

A Deepe Coffyn
A Tasty Way to Die
Hotel Morgue
Recipe for Death

NON-FICTION

A Little French Cookbook
A Little Scandinavian Cookbook
A Taste of Somerset Guide to Good Food & Drink
Just for Two

Death and the Epicure

Janet Laurence

HEADLINE

First published in 1993
by Macmillan London Limited

First published in paperback in 1994
by HEADLINE BOOK PUBLISHING PLC

10 9 8 7 6 5 4 3 2 1

ISBN 0 7472 4244 5

Printed and bound in Great Britain by
HarperCollins Manufacturing, Glasgow

HEADLINE BOOK PUBLISHING PLC
Headline House
79 Great Titchfield Street
London W1P 7FN

To Peter and Annie
With many thanks for Hong Kong

Acknowledgements

I have to thank a number of people for help in researching the background of this book. Robert Dark of Epicure Foods and John Brennan of B.E. International Foods both spent precious time giving me details of the specialist food business. Roger Lovegrove, proprietor with his wife of Martin's, Castle Cary's excellent specialist grocer, also provided valuable information. Neither Finer Foods nor the Delicatessen nor the people involved bear any resemblance to any of the above. I was entertained royally by my brother and sister-in-law, Peter and Anne Duffell, in Hong Kong, where Annie spent days showing me around. Our friend, John Paxton, produced electrical inspiration and details and told me the story of the mouse trap he had once designed. Dr Audrey Dunlop and Countess Castle Stewart helped with medical details. My husband provided me with much of the background financial and company shareholding details and, as usual, bore up nobly under the disruptions of writing. If, despite all the help and assistance, there are errors in the story, they are mine. None of the events or characters bear any resemblance to any actual event or person except by coincidence.

Chapter One

Animosity crackled round the table like caramel on crème brûlée. This was not a series of business disagreements, this was infighting of a personal kind. Darina Lisle wished she was somewhere else.

Christians *v*. lions could probably have provided the same queasy fascination. The trouble with this occasion was the impossibility of deciding who was Christian and which were the lions.

Across the table was Marian Drax, an unlikely lion. A thin woman in her early fifties, she could once have been attractive, now life had drained the sap and left dry desiccation. Blue eyes were pale as bleached denim and her skin had the colour and tone of uncooked filo pastry. Faded blonde hair swept into a French pleat seemed too heavy for her slender neck and the force in her voice was no more than the rustle of dying leaves. Her insubstantial body had at one point shaken with barely contained anger, her eyes watering dangerously, but her resentment emerged in tones of aggrieved complaint with no hint of Christian commitment. 'You run this company, Joel, as though you're a sultan ordering his harem.'

'Only natural, considering how he got to be managing director,' Anna Drax Johnson drawled from the other end of the luncheon table. Her head with its smooth cap of shining chestnut hair was held slightly on one side, her agate eyes gleamed with both enjoyment and malice. She exuded energy and a sense of power, a positive lion. Yet she had also displayed all the fervour of religious conviction.

Marian Drax glanced to her right, at the man sitting at the table's head; her thin mouth twisted uncomfortably and her body shifted in misery. 'Oh, I didn't mean, that is, let's be fair about this, Anna.'

'Yes,' said the host with an urbane charm that signalled danger

9

more potently than outright hostility; he had lion potential certainly but something else that hinted at a more devious animal. 'By all means let us be fair, Marian. Let us, for instance, ask why it is taking so long for you to come to a decision on computerizing the company accounts? One could almost imagine you are afraid an efficient system would reveal – well, what could it reveal?' He glanced round the table with an air of frank enquiry.

'For Heaven's sake, Joel, you can't be suggesting there's anything wrong with Marian's accounting system,' blustered the Sales Director on Darina's right. He shot the left cuff of his fine cambric shirt with a nervous gesture, revealing amethyst cufflinks set in gold. A man about the same age as the accountant, he had held back from the fight until now. Darina wondered whether Michael Berkeley was reluctant to choose sides or just preferred to stand outside bullet range.

There had been no such reluctance from the last member of the luncheon table. Early thirties, soberly suited, receding fair hair brushed straight back from a closed face, it had been Peter Drax who had diverted attention from consideration of the food to the company's lack of profits.

'I would like to raise the question of the decline in our profits,' he had said, enunciating each word with a precise care that suggested he strove to convey maturity beyond his years. 'I understand that our dividend will be badly down. I hope this is only a momentary aberration and not a trend that is continuing. If so,' he held up a hand to prevent any premature interruption, though none was attempted. 'If so, I would like some explanation.'

All eyes had looked at Managing Director Joel Madoc and from that moment it seemed Darina's presence had been forgotten.

'You should have become a surgeon, Peter, rather than a GP, you cut straight to the heart of the problem. Let's ask your sister. Well, Anna, as marketing director, what is your explanation?'

Lions and Christians had then fallen to tearing flesh in bloody and unwieldy chunks as argument zigzagged back and forth. Cast as spectator, Darina tried to give her attention to the food rather than accusation and counter-accusation. It was, after all, what she was there for.

The table was furnished with profligate generosity. Sufficient for many more than six guests, the dishes seemed the result of a royal plunder of some high-class delicatessen. Excellent ham, well-flavoured Continental sausages, and delicious pickled herrings prepared in various sauces were interspersed with salads of the sort Darina normally would never have given much of her attention. Harvested from tinned vegetables and dried fruits in imaginative combinations, dressed with style, they were surprisingly tasty. Whatever reservations she had about the company at this unpleasant luncheon table did not apply to the food.

Which was strange because her initial reaction to the proposed project had been reluctance to become involved with just this kind of fare.

It was Charles Johnson, her publisher, who had suggested it might be something she could be interested in.

'Finer Foods is planning a promotional campaign,' he'd said casually after they had finished discussing the cover of Darina's new cookery book. 'They want to publish a paperback as part of a move to redefine their position in the market place. You know the sort of thing, a guide to using their products, something that will display the virtuosity and underline the quality of their specialist foods, with lots of attractive recipes. Illustrated with atmospheric line drawings, we thought; class without the expense of photography.' He finished making some notes then glanced at her. 'Could you be interested, or have you something else on the go at the moment?' He might have been asking if she'd decided what to have for supper.

'Only ideas,' Darina had acknowledged.

'Well, how about it? Sort of thing you might take on?' There was no pressure behind the enquiry.

Darina considered him thoughtfully as he leaned the back of his chair negligently against the overflowing bookcase in his office. A paisley bow tie flowered at the neck of his Viyella shirt and a long cardigan was buttoned over well-tailored grey trousers; half-lenses and fair hair in need of a cut softened the asceticism of his bony face and gave him the look of a religious who'd decided the monk's cell was too uncomfortable. She'd known him a couple of years now, admired his ability to visualize a manuscript in finished form and was thrilled with how he had turned her wayward typescript into a printed design that made it a delight to look at and read.

She had also become accustomed to his low-key approach to subjects close to his heart. She wondered what had excited him about this particular project. She knew the Finer Foods products of course, largely specialist items: dried foods, continental meats, canned fruit and vegetables, preserves, ethnic sauces, all of excellent quality, but what he had just described sounded like a routine sponsored volume, hardly the kind of book that would get his publishing adrenalin going.

'I'm not sure it's my sort of cookery,' she said cautiously.

'Joel Madoc, their managing director, is a friend of mine,' Charles said with throw-away matter-of-factness. 'I'd like to see them producing something a little different, occurred to me you might be the ideal choice, your knack of producing attractive but accessible recipes with a touch of something out of the ordinary is just what they need.'

'Flattery will get you everywhere,' said Darina. But she was pleased none the less.

'Or do you find the prospect of pulses, prunes, and Parmesan boring beyond words?'

'That's too cruel,' she protested. 'I've got several of the Finer Foods items on my shelves at this moment.'

'For emergency use only?'

'Not at all.' When she thought about it, in fact, there were many of their products she used regularly; things like tinned tomatoes, lots more flavour than most of the fresh ones available in England, dried pulses for a large number of dishes, dried fruit for a variety of purposes, not to mention various of their extensive range of Chinese and Indian products. There was no excuse for her to be élitist about them. 'How long a book and what's the time scale?'

'Quite short and they want to be able to publish this time next year.' He looked at her over his half-lenses with birdlike brightness. 'Need a completed manuscript by January if possible.'

'But that only gives three months!' Darina exclaimed. But the immediacy of the project if not the subject attracted her. So she'd agreed to meet Charles's friend, Managing Director Joel Madoc, and a lunch at Finer Foods was arranged.

The company was located near Marlborough and the M4, not much more than a thirty-minute drive from Darina's home in Somerset. It was housed in a large Victorian house converted into offices with an unobtrusive extension built on what Joel Madoc explained to her had once been the tennis court and croquet lawn.

'There are times certain members of the firm wish they still existed, the work ethic here at the moment leaves something to be desired.' The biting edge to his voice should have warned her luncheon could be less than congenial.

Joel Madoc looked like a bulldog after a facelift. Immaculate grooming gave his heavy jaw and square mouth a smooth charm. Greying hair with a strong curl, cut *en brosse*, emphasized the strength of his head. His trim body was clothed in a suit of stunningly unobtrusive elegance offset by a shirt that clamoured for approbation, its stripes a beguiling melange of terracotta, blue, and apricot that required an Italian sun for full appreciation of the effect.

He had taken her hand in both of his, pressing it with urgent warmth, and brown as toast eyes looked deeply into hers, unembarrassed by the fact that her nearly six foot plus the high heels she was wearing gave her several inches' advantage over him. 'Charles has told me lots about you and I am looking forward so much to your book coming out, cooking for two is just what I need.' His voice had a liquid richness that poured over Darina like fudge sauce over ice-cream.

Somewhat bemused, Darina had allowed herself to be taken on a brief tour of the Finer Foods offices. It was all modern efficiency in the extension and spacious charm in the original house, where the board room and chief offices were located. Her tour included an attractive kitchen fitted into the former library, used, the Managing Director explained, for experimenting with new and existing products.

Finally Joel Madoc had opened the door into the company dining room to introduce Darina to the other directors.

There was sudden silence as they entered the room. The group of two women and one man gathered around the fireplace stood awkwardly, like children caught in some forbidden activity. Then Anna Drax Johnson moved smoothly forward and Darina forgot that first impression. Almost immediately afterwards Peter Drax had entered with apologies for his lateness and the party was complete.

Darina had been introduced to Anna, the marketing director, to Marian, financial director, and Michael, sales director. There had been no explanatory title when Peter Drax's turn had come; he appeared to be a non-executive director.

After his enquiry into the company's financial position all the directors appeared to forget they had a guest with them at the luncheon table, and as the in-fighting got under way Darina wondered if Charles Johnson was aware that Finer Foods had financial problems. He certainly hadn't mentioned any such possibility to her. All he had said was that the company felt a need to raise its profile as market leader in specialist foods in the face of increasing competition.

It seemed, though, that the company had problems more serious than a proliferation of competing products.

As marketing director, Anna delivered her analysis of the situation with fervent conviction and a biting sarcasm for what she saw as Joel's ignorance. According to her, the answer to their difficulties lay in the company entering the supermarket field. 'That could greatly increase our sales. Our future has to lie where the modern consumer buys his food. The days of patronizing the local grocer and delicatessen have gone, no one has time for that sort of shopping any more.'

'Finer Foods has built its reputation on exclusivity, on the loyalty of specialist outlets,' Joel said quietly.

'Most of which are dying on their feet.'

'Then there's display, we would have no control over that at all, it could be disastrous.'

'If you ever bothered to visit a modern store you would see their display is every bit as attractive as that in your so-called exclusive grocer, more so than many. They have delicatessen and wet-fish counters, their butchery is leading the market, and who has been introducing new fruit and vegetables to the consumer? Not your local greengrocer.'

'Haven't you seen how their growth curves have flagged lately? Seen the pressure for profits, the increase in cut-price warehouse-type stores? Is that where you want to see Finer Foods? I know you have very little understanding of our products as food, but—'

Anna shot him a look compounded of venom and resentment and broke in before he could malign her further. 'I know a great deal more about our products than you and I know beyond doubt that your idea for starting a chain of delicatessens is a bankruptcy maker before the first one is open.'

That was when the vitriol started to flow in earnest with Marian and Peter being drawn into Anna's battle with the managing director.

Darina couldn't help admiring Joel Madoc's ability to keep his composure. However personal the insults, his voice never rose, his manner remained calm. The more outrageous the accusation, the quieter he became. But when Michael Berkeley sprang to Marian Drax's defence after his suggestion she might have an ulterior motive for hesitating in her choice of computer, he laid down his knife and fork with all the deliberation of a boxer stripping himself for action.

'Let me make one thing perfectly plain. The dip in the company profits concerns me as much as it does all of you. As a newcomer, I cannot accept responsibility, but I am determined to identify the cause. Your figures, Anna and Michael, suggest that it is not due to a marked drop in turnover. I have looked at such other figures as Marian has been able to produce but there is insufficient information at the moment to prove anything.'

He looked round the table at the wary faces regarding him. 'Without detailed, up-to-date statistics, we are lost. That is why I am so anxious to get through this nightmare, and I do understand,' he said, turning towards Marian Drax, 'that to you the computerizing of our accounts must be that. But the alternative must be an even greater nightmare, both to the company and to you personally. If you haven't been able to choose and order a computer by the end of the month, we shall have to appoint a financial director who can.'

There was stunned silence. No doubt about who was lion and who Christian now. Marian Drax sat with the last remnants of her colour draining away. Her mouth opened and shut like a fish wordlessly gasping for air. She looked at Anna Drax Johnson for support. It came.

'You can't do that, Joel. This is a family company, Marian is a shareholder as well as financial director.'

'Until you can command the support of more than fifty per cent of the shares,' he said silkily, 'I think my decisions must prevail.'

Anna bit her lip and one clenched hand pressed hard against the polished mahogany of the table.

'If you would only accept our offer to buy you out, Joel, your problems would be solved.'

'No hope, my dear. This company was left to me to run and run it I will.'

'Even though it is into the ground?'

It was Peter Drax who defused the situation. 'I must say, Anna, I have to agree with Joel and I can't see what Marian is getting so worked up about. We have everything at the surgery on computer and it's amazing how it has clarified all sorts of situations for us. We know exactly how much each aspect of the practice is costing and can compare the figures with those of the previous week or month or year.' He leaned towards the pale woman sitting on his right. 'I know you've done a wonderful job over the years, Marian, but times have changed.'

She looked back at him, her pale blue eyes a mixture of consternation and distress, tried to speak, failed to find the necessary control, dropped her napkin on her plate, and hurriedly left the table.

Michael Berkeley half rose. Anna laid a hand on his arm, 'Let her go, you can't help.' He sank back into his seat.

Then it seemed that Joel at last recollected his guest. 'My dear Darina, how very bad mannered of us to display all our dirty linen in public. These should be matters for the board room, not the luncheon table. I hardly dare ask now if you are prepared to take on this assignment?'

'I think it would be impossible to produce something satisfactory to you all,' Darina said slowly to the table at general. 'There seem too many differences in outlook.'

'Don't worry about me,' said Anna, her colour high as she sat painfully erect and self-contained. 'I agreed with the idea when it was first mooted. Indeed, it is one of the few ideas being produced at the moment with which I do agree.'

'Right!' said Michael Berkeley heartily, appearing to leap at the possibility of a non-contentious subject. 'I have been saying for some time we need just such a book, something that would underline our commitment to quality, explain our products are . . .' he hesitated and looked appealingly towards Anna for help.

Unexpectedly, it came from the Managing Director. 'Something that will explain our products are as valid for good cooking as freshly picked vegetables or properly hung meat; are essential in the kitchens of all good and adventurous cooks. That is the message we want to get over. Michael, take Miss Lisle into the board room and run through our range.' He turned to Darina. 'I will arrange for coffee to be brought to you there.' There was no hint of choice in the suggestion.

Whether she wanted to or not, Darina was to learn more about Finer Foods and its products.

Chapter Two

Michael Berkeley led Darina across the reception hall and into the board room.

It was handsomely proportioned, its walls lined with glass-fronted shelves displaying the company's product ranges, all emblazoned with the distinctive Finer Foods logo.

The Sales Director opened a cupboard and took out some brochures. 'The company began life as a specialist grocers in the nineteenth century,' he started.

But Darina wasn't listening. She moved to the head of the long mahogany table, drew out the heavy armchair obviously designed for the chairman of the board, and seated herself. 'I think you had better fill me in on exactly why the Managing Director does not seem to have the confidence of his chief executives.'

He hesitated, narrow shoulders drooping under a skilfully padded jacket. 'I don't think—' he began.

'Look, Joel Madoc could have stopped that display in there, I can't call it a discussion, at any time. It was quite obvious he wanted me to know all about the company and his position in it. Why else were we sent in here?'

The Sales Director's face lost its pleasant amiability, it was as though he found himself facing a *viva voce* for a subject he hadn't studied. He waved a hand half-heartedly at the glass shelves then squared his shoulders, resettling the shoulder pads, and drew out a chair half-way down the table. He sat, took off his glasses, polished and replaced them on his straight, well-shaped nose, dropped his pile of company brochures on the polished wood, and fiddled until they were aligned in a neat pile parallel to the edge of the table. Darina waited patiently.

'Let me help,' she said at last as it seemed he was unable to work out where to start. 'When and how did Joel Madoc become managing director of Finer Foods?'

The Sales Director was still in some difficulty. He laid his arms carefully on the table, clasped his hands, looked down, unclasped the hands, twisted his signet ring, and finally said, 'It was the wish of his wife, Eleanor Drax.' He looked up at Darina. 'She was the one who really made Finer Foods. Her father, Harvey Drax, acquired it after the Second World War.' His voice gradually gained confidence. 'He expanded the ranges, started selling to Chinese restaurants, and they still make up a sizeable segment of our business, but it was Eleanor who created the brand image, got the sales force moving, and provided the inspiration that made us the thriving company we are today.'

A well-rehearsed little speech, Darina thought, that brought her not much closer to understanding what had been going on at lunch.

'Eleanor Drax? What relation are Marian, Peter, and Anna to her.'

'Marian's her sister, Peter and Anna are both her children.' Michael Berkeley produced the facts quite happily.

'But Joel Madoc isn't their father.' It was a statement, not a query. Apart from the difference in surname, which meant nothing in itself since even his wife seemed to have called herself Drax, the Managing Director looked some years short of fifty and Anna Drax Johnson was pushing hard at forty, with her brother probably five or so years younger.

Michael Berkeley ran a finger along the edge of his neat pile of brochures. 'Anna and Peter's father died just over twenty years ago, Anna was about eighteen.'

'A difficult age for a girl to lose her father.' Darina knew just how difficult it was. 'Did you know him?'

'Not really, I hadn't been with the firm long and Patrick Cavanagh was hardly ever seen in the offices.'

'Cavanagh? Didn't Eleanor Drax use her first husband's name either?'

'I gather it was some stipulation of the old man's. Patrick Cavanagh, well, let's just say he wasn't a great success as a business man. Harvey Drax had little time for people who weren't a success.' He glanced at a picture above the fireplace. Darina followed his gaze. A heavy-featured man with cold eyes looked across at her. His determined mouth had been inherited by his granddaughter. Darina felt the air grow slightly chill.

Then she noticed another portrait that had to be of Eleanor

Drax. Even allowing for artistic flattery, she had been a spectacularly beautiful woman. Very like her sister, the same fair hair, oval face, and slender neck, but exuding the vitality her daughter displayed and her sister lacked, or had lost over the years. Had it been the vitality or the looks that had enabled her to capture and hold a man so much younger than herself? Perhaps it was the combination that had proved so seductive.

'So Joel Madoc was Eleanor Drax's second husband. How long ago did they marry?'

Michael Berkeley thought for a moment. 'Must be about sixteen years.'

'Sixteen?' Darina could hear the surprise in her voice.

'Something like that. But it was only recently he became involved with the company.'

'Someone else who wasn't very successful?' murmured Darina, but she was thinking that that couldn't be the reason. Whatever else Joel Madoc was, she couldn't see him as any sort of failure, he wore confidence and power as only someone who has conquered time after time can, or is perhaps a first-class con man. Now where had that thought come from? It was so alien that Darina was astonished at herself.

'Joel Madoc was a success all right,' confirmed Michael Berkeley. 'He built up his own men's fashion company, sold it last year, I believe very advantageously.'

'What made him sell it?' Darina wondered if the money had been the attraction.

'Eleanor wanted him in the company. She was ill, I think she knew it was terminal.' Michael Berkeley hesitated a moment. 'But I think she felt she had more time, would be able to see him safely in control before she had to give up. As it was,' he cleared his throat, fiddled with the brochures again, 'she went into hospital shortly after she had appointed him managing director, then died a few weeks later, about seven months ago. It was a terrible shock to us all. And when the will was read, it turned out she'd left him her shares.'

There was a little silence. Darina thought of the other two women she had met that day, Eleanor's sister and daughter. 'How long have Marian and Anna worked with the company?' she asked.

The Sales Director sighed. 'Marian is Harvey Drax's younger daughter. Apparently Harvey insisted she join the financial side

19

as soon as she left technical college, she studied business practice and book-keeping, she isn't a fully-fledged accountant. But she has done an excellent job since taking over after her uncle's death,' he added hastily. 'We have never had any trouble with the auditors.' Darina wondered how much that meant in financial terms and waited for him to continue.

'Anna joined us about six years ago,' he said after a moment. 'Originally she trained in the fashion field, was a buyer for one of the big stores. She gave up work after the birth of her daughters. After her divorce Eleanor suggested she came into the company, she said we needed someone with Anna's design sense and retailing background to handle the marketing side.'

'But when she knew she couldn't continue to run Finer Foods herself, Eleanor Drax brought in her husband rather than hand over to either her sister or daughter?'

Michael Berkeley said nothing, he didn't need to. Darina wondered if Eleanor Drax had had sufficient energy to try and defuse the potentially explosive situation her decision had caused. If she had, judging from lunchtime, her attempt had been less than successful. Was this, then, a personal vendetta, a power struggle, or were Anna and Marian fighting in the best interests of the company?

'How much experience does Joel Madoc have?'

'As I said, he's run his own company with some success but until he started here I don't think he had had anything much to do with food, as a business.' His mouth twisted wryly. 'He does regard himself as something of an epicure, though, really enjoys good food.'

Epicure could also be used to describe someone who enjoyed sensual pleasures other than food, Darina reflected silently, then said, 'And he would no doubt have been told a good deal about Finer Foods by his wife over the years?'

Michael Berkeley shifted in his chair. 'I suppose he must have picked up something somewhere about the business. He's certainly thrown his weight around, that is, he's seemed confident enough since he started running things.'

'But if I understood what went on during lunch Finer Foods is in trouble. Is this proposed book and marketing campaign intended to do a more radical job than brighten up the company's image?'

The Sales Director adjusted his silk tie and sat a little straighter.

'There's nothing wrong with the company's image that a few more salesmen couldn't deal with. Instead of spending money on a delicatessen or the packaging needed to enter the supermarket world, we would be better off hiring more reps.'

Darina filed the comment away with others garnered during the lunchtime confrontation. She wanted to ask Michael Berkeley where he stood in all this but knew any attempt would be uselessly intrusive. If he had managed to maintain his on-the-fence posture throughout lunch, he was unlikely to come off it now for her.

Instead, she enquired how he felt about the company.

Michael Berkeley's face lightened. 'Before I started here I was a successful salesman but I had never been able to connect properly with any of my products. Finer Foods was a revelation.' So might Sir Galahad have spoken of the Holy Grail.

'You're interested in food?'

Darina had no need to ask more. She listened with interested sympathy and some carefully disguised amusement to him describing the part food played in his life.

It turned out his mother had travelled widely, first with his father then his step-father, both civil engineers, and enjoyed studying the cooking of whatever country she found herself living in.

'I learned about the world in terms of food,' said Michael Berkeley dreamily. 'India meant spices to me. China divided itself into regional cuisines, Brazil was coffee, chocolate, and manioc, a staple tuber made into bread or cooked like potato, you never see it over here, perhaps it's too bland for Western tastes and there aren't enough immigrants to create their own market, but my mother loved experimenting with it.'

Darina thought that here was a woman she could relate to and asked if she was still alive, wondering if it would be possible to meet her.

'Yes, but we don't have much to do with each other.' He looked out of the window at the autumnal shrubs. 'I hated my step-father, he returned the compliment, and I thought my mother cared more for my half-brother than for me. As soon as I was grown up, I severed all relations.'

Darina decided that, despite his conciliatory approach, Michael Berkeley was as capable of deep prejudice as any member of that luncheon table.

'But after my step-father's death a few years ago, I began to see something of her again. She lives in Suffolk now.' His tone was dismissive and Darina could see there would be little point in trying to pursue her curiosity about this woman who knew so much about foreign food. She thought it was a pity mother and son couldn't have used their common enthusiasm to overcome their differences better. Then wondered about Anna's relationship with her mother. How far had the antagonism between her and Joel poisoned the filial bond? And just what lay behind that antagonism anyway? Another question it would be useless to ask this man.

'Do you spend much time travelling to discover new products?' she asked, getting the conversation back to Finer Foods.

Michael Berkeley gave a wry smile and shrugged his shoulders. 'That, I'm afraid, is not how we operate. When I started I dreamt of constant trips abroad but we rely mainly on foreign agents to bring us ideas, find suppliers and maintain quality control at the production end.' Darina listened to details of the care Finer Foods took to make sure they only marketed the best possible quality products, how strict their standards were, how detailed the specifications given to their suppliers and how they had even begun to include ecological standards as far as was possible in both production and packaging.

'How about running through the various lines with me?' she suggested at last. Michael Berkeley handed across the first of his brochures with undisguised relief at being able to get away from the company's problems, both financial and personal.

Chapter Three

Towards the end of the afternoon, Darina was delivered back to Joel Madoc's office, a spacious room panelled in dark wood.

Finer Foods' managing director was sitting at an antique partner's desk set sideways on to a bay window. No doubt Harvey Drax had sat there opposite his daughter. After his death, had she sat there alone? Until her husband had joined her for that short period of time before her own death? Could he now see an elegant ghost in the other chair?

What his gaze was actually fixed on was a large account book, but immediately they entered the room, Joel Madoc was on his feet, his charm at full battery strength.

'Come in, come in. I hope Michael has filled you in on the company and its products?' Darina had no doubts as to exactly what he meant. She assured him the Sales Director's briefing had been comprehensive.

He led the way over to a small seating area furnished with tartan-covered armchairs and a sofa, waved Darina to a seat, neatly dismissed the other man, and sat himself down. Clasping his hands lightly between his knees, he leaned forward and gave his guest his full attention. After the company of the colourless sales director, the effect was as if pure oxygen had just been poured into a rarefied atmosphere.

'Now, I hope you are prepared to take on the writing of this little book,' he began, only to be interrupted by the ringing of his telephone. He rose with an exclamation of annoyance. 'Maggie, I thought I told you to hold all calls while I have Miss Lisle with me.' Then his face beamed with delight. 'Of course you're right, I'm sorry, send her in immediately.' He replaced the receiver and turned back to Darina. 'There's someone I want you to meet.'

The door opened and a small woman entered with a little, breathless rush. She was about the same age as Anna Drax John-

23

son but where Anna was straight and implacable, the newcomer looked soft and pliant. Where Anna was all gloss and shine, this woman had fly-away hair and a plump face dominated by a pair of large and very blue eyes that were alight with excitement as Joel greeted her. It was only a brief kiss on her cheek and an arm placed around her shoulders but he invested both gestures with such obvious feeling he might just as well have passionately embraced her.

'Come and meet Darina Lisle, darling. Darina, let me introduce Jane Leslie, she runs a highly successful delicatessen.'

The newcomer smiled at Darina. 'I've been looking forward to meeting you ever since Joel said you might be writing the Finer Foods book,' she said, her voice soft and dancing with the same breathless quality as her movements. 'I always read your column in the *Recorder*, I just love your recipes. I use one of your salads in the shop, you must come over and see what we do there. Oh, do let's sit, I've been standing all day.' She plumped herself down on the sofa and placed a plastic bag on the table in front of her. Any elegant ghost occupying the other seat at the partner's desk had been banished from the room.

Joel sat beside the newcomer and opened the bag without ceremony. 'What have you got in here? Some new goodies you've found? Jane is one of my chief spies among the opposition,' he said to Darina. 'She's always bringing me samples of something I ought to see.' He pulled out a bottle of Chinese soy sauce, placed it on the table and stared at it. 'But it's one of ours!'

'Taste it,' ordered Jane Leslie.

Joel Madoc shook the bottle, unscrewed its top, poured a little of the contents onto the tip of his finger and licked it assessingly. The two women watched as he considered the flavour. He picked up the bottle again and studied the label. 'Something wrong with that, definitely.' He put it back on the table and stared at it once more.

'One of my regulars brought it back today, said she thought it must be old stock or something. I tasted it and, just like you, thought it wasn't at all right. So I decided to bring it along, thought you wouldn't mind my turning up early.'

Joel hardly seemed to notice her smile. He rose and went to the telephone.

A few minutes later a young man Darina remembered being introduced to her as the Quality Control Manager came into the office.

Joel Madoc wasted little time on pleasantries. 'I thought we tested every consignment that came into the warehouse?'

'Almost everything, yes.' The young man looked worried.

'What do you mean, almost everything?' The dangerously controlled tone had the manager nervously shifting his weight from one foot to the other.

'Well, that is, there are certain completely reliable lines we don't bother with.'

'I thought I'd given directions every batch of every product was to be sampled.'

The young man now looked positively unhappy. 'Well, sir, Miss Drax Johnson said you obviously didn't mean those products we'd never had to sample in the past, sir.'

'Like this one, I suppose?' Joel Madoc held out the bottle of soy sauce, his eyes hooded.

The bottle was taken from him. 'Yes, that's one of the lines. It's one of our best sellers, produced under highly controlled conditions in China, one of their most modern factories. Hong Kong runs a quality check, of course, and we've never had any trouble with it.'

'Well, you've got trouble now. Taste it.'

Once again the bottle was shaken and the sauce assessed. The Quality Control Manager's expression changed from worry to shock. 'I, I don't know what to say, sir. This is dreadful, I can't think what's happened.'

'Go and check the batch number and then get on to Hong Kong and ask them what the hell's going on. And get Sales to check who the rest of the batch went to and recall it. And, Walters, from now on everything gets sampled, right?'

'Right, sir, right! I'll get on to it right away.' The man scuttered away like a rabbit disappearing out of the sight lines of a farmer's gun.

Joel Madoc watched him leave the office then reached for the telephone again. 'Tell Miss Drax Johnson I want to see her in here, immediately.' The receiver was jammed back and Joel rejoined Darina and Jane Leslie. A little pulse at the corner of his jaw was beating hard. Jane took his hand as he sat beside her but said nothing.

Darina rose. 'I think I should leave you to sort all this out. Why don't I give you a ring tomorrow?'

'Please, don't go,' said Joel, 'I shan't be tied up long. Jane, my darling, why don't you take Darina to have a look at the kitchen?

25

She'd probably be interested to see where we concoct recipes to try our products, I don't think she got more than a glimpse of it before.'

The two women left the office just as Anna Drax Johnson swept in, ignoring both of them. Jane Leslie carefully closed the door behind her and led the way across the hall to the kitchen.

A young man was working at the stove, stir-frying with deep concentration, tossing a mixture of various fruits and stem ginger over a high flame. As Darina watched, he cleared the bottom of the wok and added a sauce, stirring swiftly as it thickened slightly and cleared, then mixing it in with the fruit. He gave Jane Leslie a brief greeting, reserving his main attention for his dish.

'An entry for the competition, John?' The cook gave a quick grin and nodded. He reached for a plate and, with a swift movement, decanted the contents of the wok. He found some forks and offered his dish.

'Have a try, tell me what you think.'

'Delicious,' pronounced Darina after trying the hot fruit and ginger. 'The Marsala in the sauce is wonderful.'

'Excellent,' agreed Jane Leslie, but her mind was obviously not on the food. With a visible effort she injected some enthusiasm into her voice. 'That must stand a good chance of winning.'

The cook shrugged ruefully. 'I don't know, everyone is getting really keen, the kitchen's booked up for days ahead.'

Darina asked what sort of competition it was.

'Joel has asked everyone to come up with new ideas for using the company products,' Jane explained. Darina wondered whether she was going to be expected to incorporate some of the recipes into her book. It could be a good idea and save her some work; if, that is, she took on the project.

There was much that disturbed Darina about Finer Foods but much that intrigued her as well. Including this woman, who appeared to have comforted the grieving widower in a remarkably short time.

In Joel Madoc's office Jane Leslie had radiated happiness; away from him she seemed forlorn. Her face fell into lines of unhappiness, her full little mouth lost its swollen smile and drooped, her huge eyes acquired a quality of remoteness, an inability to connect with others. Her words suggested an interest that her manner denied. Were she a romantic, Darina thought, she would say Jane trailed mystery like a Wilkie Collins heroine. But being instead a practical person, she turned her attention back to the competition.

26

'What's first prize?'

'A trip to Hong Kong with a visit to China to see ginger growing. Who will you take if you win, John?' Again there was that wandering glance that denied any real involvement.

'Catch Sharon allowing me to take anyone but her!' he grinned at them.

'Wedding bells ringing yet?' For the first time Jane Leslie sounded genuinely interested.

'Nah, she says we've got to save up for a house first. With the prices so low now, though, reckon it won't be long. Well, I'd better wash these things, my time's nearly up.' He busied himself clearing away. There was a dishwasher but it sported a large notice Not For Employees' Use and the young man washed all his utensils in the twin sinks before returning to his office clutching the piece of paper on which he'd written his recipe.

Darina looked round the kitchen, admiring the combination of well-chosen equipment, ample working surfaces, and old library shelves holding a collection of cookery books interspersed with copper moulds and kitchen memorabilia.

'I understand Anna was responsible for giving it a facelift a couple of years ago. I can't fault her design sense.' Jane wrinkled her nose in a telling gesture of distaste. Anna was obviously not her flavour of the month. Then she smiled, her face transformed once more to that of a happy woman. 'Joel allows any member of the staff to use the kitchen for a couple of sessions a week to work on their recipes, he's so keen everyone gets as involved with what Finer Foods means to the customer as he is himself. He's really dedicated to the business.'

'Is that why he's so keen the company has its own delicatessen?'

'One of the reasons,' Joel Madoc said behind them. 'I also want to have total control over display, not to have to see our products hidden on the bottom shelf or Indian chutneys muddled up with Chinese sauces. I want a store that looks like a cook's promised land, every shelf a treasure trove with every item given its proper value. And I want to be able to show how versatile so many of our products can be.'

'You don't think my delicatessen's good enough for you?' Jane Leslie teased him, the breathless joy back in her voice.

'Without it I would never have learned the business so fast.' He put his arm around her and pulled the small body against his.

'How did your confrontation with Anna go?' She looked at him with worried eyes.

'Surprisingly well, considering how antagonistic she was at lunch. She actually admitted it was a mistake to amend my sampling order.'

'But surely that was just another attempt to undermine your authority?'

'Do you know, I'm not sure it was? She said she just assumed I couldn't have meant to include products that had proved themselves so reliable that it would be counter-productive in terms of time and money.'

'Honestly, Joel, sometimes I think I should be jealous of the way you always give Anna the benefit of the doubt.'

'Never!' He held her even closer.

'You couldn't confine your sexual excesses to outside office hours, I suppose?' drawled Anna Drax Johnson as she entered the kitchen carrying a tray laden with various ingredients.

Jane Leslie flushed and attempted to move away from Joel but he held her firmly.

'I'm sure you will want to be the first to offer your congratulations,' he said to Anna as she laid her tray on the work surface by the stove. 'Jane and I are engaged.'

There was silence. Anna Drax Johnson remained for a split second with her back to the happy couple, her hands busy with removing things from her tray. Only Darina could see that they trembled. Then she turned. 'That's wonderful, I hope you'll be very happy.' A smile was firmly glued to her face, she managed to sound genuinely pleased, then she looked beyond her step-father to the door. The Financial Director was standing there, a sheaf of papers in her hand. 'Isn't it wonderful,' Anna said, with something in her voice that suggested it was anything but, 'Joel and Jane have just got engaged.'

Marian Drax stood motionless, looking from Joel to Jane to Anna. 'Wonderful.' She repeated the word as though it belonged to a foreign language. 'Wonderful.' This time she tried for more emphasis, then her face contorted into rage. Unexpected strength flowed into her. 'Wonderful?' she repeated again with scorn. 'It's impossible! You'll never marry that woman, not after I've finished!' As suddenly as it had arrived, her powerful emotion vanished, her face crumpled, the beginnings of a wail was strangled and she turned, stumbling slightly. Then, for the second time that day, Darina saw Finer Foods' financial director leave the room in tears.

'Well!' said Anna Drax Johnson. She sounded unpleasantly pleased. 'What can she mean? What has been going on, dear Joel?'

Her step-father stood silent, his arm wrapped tightly around his fiancée, his expression unreadable. Jane Leslie looked deeply shocked.

Chapter Four

'So, you're going to do the book,' had been William's comment after Darina had given him an insult by insult account of her lunch.

'Yes. The contract's reasonably generous, the products are good, and it shouldn't take me long. Just the sort of thing I need to keep me out of mischief before we decide when we're getting married.' She looked up from scrubbing potatoes and grinned happily at her fiancé as he laid the table for their supper.

'I'd like to think that means you're prepared to set an early date but I'm afraid you're just fascinated by what sounds like a right royal battle between this Madoc chap and his step-daughter.'

'How well you know me.' Darina put the potatoes on to boil and turned her attention towards making a salad, carefully cleaning various pieces of greenery garnered from their small garden.

'It looks as though I have a diet of delicatessen fare to look forward to.' The prospect did not seem to daunt him.

'If you don't enjoy it, I'll be failing. Try this hummus, I've used a tin of Finer Foods' chick peas, much quicker than cooking them from scratch.' Darina put a dish of the Middle Eastern garlic-laden pâté on the table with thick slices of crusty bread. Her fiancé attacked it with appetite and manifest approval.

'Carry on this way and you won't hear a word of objection from me; but if the company is in real trouble, won't you be in danger of not being paid for the book?'

It was a point that hadn't occurred to Darina. She thought briefly. 'I shall have a third of the fee up front, another third when I deliver the manuscript. I think those bits are probably safe enough. But I would back Joel Madoc to straighten out whatever trouble there is. Anna Drax Johnson may make a lot of noise but he comes over as someone who wins out every time.'

Darina set the salad on one side and arranged a couple of

salmon steaks in an oblong dish. 'Now that's enough of my doings, what's been happening with you?' She scattered chopped herbs and a spoonful of white wine over her fish and covered it all with clingfilm. Receiving no response to her query, she looked across at her fiancé. William, what's been going on? You look . . .' She studied him more closely. 'You look like a moggy who's been presented with a dish, no, a *pond* of unpasteurized cream.'

Her fiancé's aura of self-satisfaction deepened. Indeed, he positively purred but he said nothing.

'Darling, you don't mean, you haven't, I mean, you aren't, are you?'

He nodded.

Darina gave a screech of joy. 'I don't believe it! And you said nothing, how could you?'

'Well, you were so excited about all the strange people you'd met today, I thought my news could wait.'

'As though I wouldn't have been far more interested to hear that you are now Detective Inspector Pigram of the CID! Oh, where's the champagne?'

William propelled his long legs in the direction of the fridge. 'I put a bottle in as soon as I got back. That's another reason I waited with the news, to give it time to chill a bit. Hope it's had long enough.'

'Oh, don't worry about the temperature, open it, let's drink to your promotion.'

She watched him skilfully twist the champagne bottle, rather than the cork, until a subdued pop released the precious contents and he poured them both a glass. She raised hers. 'Here's to my hero, the newest detective inspector in the Avon and Somerset Police Force. At least, is it the Avon and Somerset, or shall we be moving elsewhere?'

Darina knew William was keen to transfer to London, where he felt the action was. And if that was the case they would be able to live in her Chelsea house. Although she would be sorry to leave Somerset, and fond as she was of their cottage, she missed the comfort and style of the home she'd inherited from her cousin. There were many reasons to welcome a return there.

Darina looked at her fiancé, tried to read the answer in his face and only found the same mixed emotions she felt herself. 'Well? Come on, don't keep it to yourself. You know all that really matters to me is that we are together.'

'We're staying here. That's where the vacancy is, I hope you're not disappointed?'

'Not me,' said Darina with conviction. 'But didn't you want a transfer to the Met?'

'Rather to my surprise, I'm pleased to be staying. It could be something to do with the fact I've realized there's nearly as much mayhem on our doorstep as there is in London. Or that I would hate to exchange our quality of life here for the concrete jungle. Or that I'm so thrilled with the promotion I don't mind where it is.'

'Well, I'm glad it isn't in some industrial town with dreadful weather.'

William offered to refill Darina's glass but she shook her head. 'Let's save the rest to have with supper. Have you told your parents? Well, why don't you give them a ring now, the potatoes still need a few minutes and I can pop the salmon in the microwave when you've finished. They are going to be thrilled with the news.'

Darina couldn't have been more delighted herself with William's promotion. He had so much to offer. Not only a sharp intelligence but also a quiet understanding of people and an ability to get the best out of them. It wasn't only that, though. Since they'd known each other, she was the one who had been successful, had managed to make the transition from caterer to food writer, had things going her way. It was time he had a boost as well.

Now, two weeks later, in the quiet of the Finer Foods board room, Darina checked her notes on their complete range of dried and tinned pulses and reflected that it was just as well she had this project to keep her occupied.

Her work was progressing well and Joel Madoc in particular was being very helpful. 'I'm cooking along with the rest of them,' he had told her a couple of days earlier. 'Trying to recapture some of my Italian mama's cooking.'

Several things had clicked into place for Darina. 'Do you speak Italian?' she asked.

'Si, Signorina. My brother lives in Tuscany, he runs the family vineyard and also produces superb estate-bottled olive oil, green and peppery but with subtle length; Finer Foods markets it over here, if you haven't tried it already, pour a little on good fresh bread and stand at the gates of heaven as you savour it.'

'But you went into fashion rather than wine?'

'That was my father's influence. He was a painter, came from Wales. He met my mother during the war. It was one of those romantic encounters, young Italian girl hides wounded soldier who returns after the hostilities to persuade her to marry him. Finally she did.'

'You make it sound as though he had something of a task.'

'She'd heard that England was grey and cold with terrible food. But father pursued her with such passion she couldn't resist.' Joel gave a wolfish grin. 'She always insisted that was the start of his advertising career.'

'Did she ever regret giving up the Italian sun and food?'

'*Dio mio*, yes. She hated the English reserve and pomposity. Said they were all hypocrites. When my father complained that he was Welsh, she shouted that they were worse. My parents were always fighting; over his affairs, her trips back to Italy, his neglect of the family, her possessiveness; finally it all broke up and Mama went back to Tuscany with my brother.'

'And you stayed with your father?'

'Well, I was starting at design college. No, I must be honest, I think I would have stayed with Dad anyway. He was,' Joel hesitated for a moment then said, 'I think wonderfully robust is the only way to describe him. He made life constantly exciting, I could quite understand how he got Mama to marry him.'

'But she couldn't get him to remain faithful?'

Again that wolfish grin. 'It would have been like asking a bull to keep to one heifer!' There was no answer to that.

'But you kept in touch with your mother?'

'Of course! We loved each other very much. And she was such a wonderful cook, I could never have given up her food. What risottos, what polenta, her pasta! If I could manage anything near those, I'd win the competition, no trouble. But I have to rule myself ineligible, of course.' For a moment he looked sincerely regretful.

'We can always put them in the book, though,' Darina said.

'Really, you mean that?'

'Only if they are as good as you say,' she replied sternly, amused at his childlike pleasure at the suggestion and intrigued at how quickly he could change moods. When she had entered his office he had been castigating poor Marina Drax, who apparently had still not made a decision on the new accounting procedures. Now the dangerous lion had turned into a playful tabby. Italian blood crossed with Welsh had to be a perfect recipe for a mercurial temperament but it didn't sound as if either of his parents had donated that additional stray gene that made it possible for him to maintain his cool under pressure, to ignore personal attacks, the way he had done during that first lunch. It was almost sinister how he could metamorphose sparkling charm into a steely control that betrayed nothing of what he was feeling. Darina wondered if Jane Leslie had ever been shown the way he could manipulate people, the coldness that could alienate as easily as the charm could enchant.

In the fortnight since her promotion, Darina had hardly seen William. All his time seemed to be taken up with mastering the details of various cases he had inherited. They'd had to cancel a weekend arranged to visit his parents. Which had been something of a relief to Darina. An evening spent with her future parents-in-law just after the engagement had been announced had been pleasant but left her with a shrewd suspicion that William's mother, however delighted she professed to be, felt her son could have found a more suitable partner in life. Since then there had been several phone calls from Mrs Pigram with masterful suggestions on wedding plans.

Darina pushed any thought of her mother-in-law-to-be on one side and attempted to concentrate on her task, only to be interrupted by Maggie, the receptionist, asking if she would mind a visitor waiting in the board room. She ushered in a man in his early forties wearing a Burberry that looked as though it had only just been removed from the shop's hanger.

'Patrick Browne, with an "e",' he introduced himself, his manner as crisp as his coat.

She found herself shaking his outstretched hand and giving him her name in return.

'I've an appointment with Joel Madoc, just flown in from Hong Kong.' The newcomer placed an expensive-looking briefcase neatly on the board-room table and sat down, opening his trench coat and feeling in his jacket pocket for a packet of cigarettes.

Darina refused his offer of one. 'From Hong Kong? You must be jet lagged. Shouldn't you be recovering from the flight, not making business calls? I suppose it is business?'

'I'm the new Finer Foods agent there,' he said and looked at his watch. 'I wonder where he is, I've got a crowded schedule.' He tapped irritably on the table. 'I rang from the airport to confirm my flight was on time and I understood he would be available more or less all morning.'

'He was working in the kitchen earlier, I know,' Darina said.

Patrick Browne stubbed out his half-smoked cigarette, got up and opened the door to the hall. The receptionist was on the telephone. She gave him a little wave and shook her head. He sat down again, leaving the door open so he could keep an eye on her, took out another cigarette, hesitated, then returned it to the packet and thrust both hands deep into the pockets of his trench coat.

'I'm sure Joel won't be long,' Darina said soothingly. 'Have you been offered a cup of coffee?'

'What? Oh, yes, thank you. But I drank a lot of mineral water on the plane, find liquid the best antidote to jet lag. That and sleeping.'

'You travel a lot, I suppose?'

'Have done. Was in the Army until six months ago, seemed to spend a lot of my life in aeroplanes.'

Yes, Darina could see Patrick Browne was an Army man. The neatness, the discipline, the impatience with having to hang around waiting, it all fitted her slight knowledge of the military.

The lights in the hall blinked briefly and there was a cry from Maggie. Glancing towards her desk, Darina could see the screen of her word processor was glowing with a pale, uninterrupted light. The receptionist had lost her program. 'That's the second time this morning,' she wailed. 'Just after we started the power went for twenty minutes and now look at it!' Darina's sympathy was heartfelt, power failure had more than once robbed her of precious creative work.

Patrick Browne seemed oblivious of the problem. He was back at checking his watch. Then he once again fished out his packet of cigarettes and this time lit one. 'Are you sure Mr Madoc has finished his cooking? Has anyone checked if he's still in the kitchen?'

'I'm sure Maggie would have rung through. He's probably somewhere in the warehouse, that's huge and it could take a little time to track him down. Don't worry, he'll appear soon.'

Even as she said the words, the man's unease spread to Darina. Just as she told herself not to be ridiculous, she heard Maggie give a gasp, saw her rise from her chair, her gaze fixed in the direction of the kitchen. Something urgent in the way she moved took Darina into the reception hall.

Water was seeping along the hall floor from under the kitchen door, its silent progress sinister in its remorselessness. It was like the slow flow of lava from an erupting volcano.

With Darina and the Hong Kong agent right behind her, Maggie rushed across the floor and flung open the door, then she gave a scream and stood transfixed on the threshold, both hands held to her mouth in a gesture that told of horror more graphically than any words could.

Water poured from an open tap, overflowing one of the twin sinks, cascading down the cupboard and running along the floor, its direction deflected towards the hall by the body lying on the wooden boards. A body that was stiff and rigid, the arms flung out from its sides. It was as though some great force had flung it across the room, slapping the flesh and bone down on the wooden boards into instant petrification.

Patrick Browne pushed past the two women and turned off the tap, leaning awkwardly forward to protect his coat from the water. 'Ring for an ambulance,' he instructed and flung a tea towel on to the flooded floor, where it became as instantly sodden as a sponge thrown in a swimming pool.

Maggie ran back to her desk and picked up the telephone. Darina thanked Heaven for military initiative and made herself crouch down by the body. She picked up one of the stiff wrists and felt for a pulse, couldn't find one, turned the hand over and then found herself staring at a burn seared into its heel. She turned over the other wrist and found a similar angry weal across the palm.

The power hiccup! Her knowledge of electricity was basic but the meaning of that blink suddenly seemed horrifyingly clear as she looked at the oven, a combination of gas and electricity housed in stainless steel.

Patrick Browne had found a floor cloth and bucket under the sink and was trying to mop up the flood, the skirts of his trench coat tucked around his thighs as he attempted to recapture several gallons of liquid. You could count on the Army to get on with the job in hand whatever the carnage.

'I don't think we should touch anything,' Darina said as he reached into the cupboard and brought out some dry tea towels to help soak up more liquid.

'You mean?' He looked at her and she realized he was not quite in such command as she had thought, shock glazed his eyes and his movements had a robotic stiffness.

'In the case of a sudden death like this, the police will have to investigate.'

Still holding a wet cloth, he slowly rose to his feet, water lapping round his highly polished shoes. He stood looking down at the body. 'Of course,' he murmured. 'Of course.'

'What the hell has happened?'

Joel Madoc was standing in the doorway with a crowd of curious people behind him.

Darina looked back at the body. 'I'm afraid your financial director appears to have been electrocuted,' she said.

Chapter Five

Joel Madoc took charge. He sent the curious back about their business, checked that an ambulance was on its way, then assured himself that Marian Drax showed no sign of life, checking vainly for a pulse, laying his eager ear against her chest, kneeling in the water that still lapped around the body, oblivious to his soaked trousers. At last he knelt back on his heels, closed his eyes and dragged a hand down his face, wiping out all expression. Finally he reached out and gently closed the eyes that stared out of the dead woman's agonized face.

'Tell me what happened.'

Darina gave such details as she knew.

Joel Madoc looked across at Patrick Browne, still standing by the sink, his shoes now soaked with water, his hands automatically pulling at the wet cloth with which he'd been trying to mop up. 'I was supposed to meet you this morning, wasn't I?'

The agent dropped the cloth back in the bucket. 'We can't discuss anything now, of course. What a dreadful business. I'd better remove myself and give you a ring tomorrow morning. I shall be here for a couple of days, then I'm moving on to Paris. I'll leave the details of my hotel with your receptionist.'

'Yes, yes, do that. I'm sorry, I really can't think straight at the moment.'

'Shouldn't—' Darina found her voice croaking and tried again. 'I mean, won't the police want to talk to you?' she asked.

Patrick Browne hesitated with his hand on the doorknob and looked at Joel Madoc.

'The police?' asked the Managing Director of Finer Foods.

'Won't they need to be called? It's a case of sudden death and look at her hands, they're burnt, the stove must somehow have become electrified.'

Joel Madoc gently lifted the dead woman's right hand and

looked at the scar. Then he glanced at the stove. 'I suppose,' he said reluctantly, 'you must be right. But I don't see any reason to hold up Browne. They can always contact him later.'

Darina felt William would not agree. That was the trouble with having a policeman for a fiancé, it meant you looked at certain situations in a completely different light from the average person. But she could think of no very good reason for insisting the Hong Kong agent remained. The police only needed a statement from him and, as Joel said, that could be taken later.

Joel Madoc rose to his feet and followed Patrick Browne out of the room. He ordered the receptionist to call the police then came back to stand beside Marian Drax's body, gazing down at the still caricature of a woman, the mouth drawn back in a horrific rictus. For once he seemed at something of a loss. His mouth worked for a moment, he swallowed hard and dug both hands into his trouser pockets. 'Sudden death seems to paralyse the thought processes,' he said with difficulty. 'The only other death I've been involved with was Eleanor's. That was different; it was expected, there were doctors, hospitals, treatment, final messages. This, this is so different,' he repeated. He raised his head and looked across at Darina. 'You're so calm, it's as if you dealt with this sort of thing every day.'

If only he knew how her stomach was churning, how tight a control she was having to exercise over her body. William had said once that familiarity with death never made it easier for him to face a corpse. 'It's not the first time,' she said quietly. She forbore to say how many times recently she had been faced with sudden death and not only death but murder. She turned away from that thought.

Joel Madoc didn't ask for details. Instead, he drew out a chair from the big pine table that stood in the centre of the large room, placed it beside the body, and sat. It was as if he felt he had to keep watch by his dead colleague. By his sister-in-law, Darina all at once realized. This woman had been much more than a business colleague, she was the sister of his wife, he'd known her for many years. Unbidden, the way he'd given her the ultimatum at lunch returned: computerize the accounts or go. And then there had been the curt way she'd heard him speak to her on the telephone the other day.

'I think I'd like to have a little time with her on my own,' he said.

'I'm sorry, I don't think you should be left here alone.'

'For God's sake,' anger spitted out. 'Can't you understand? We may have had our differences but she meant a lot to me.'

'I do understand.' Darina was embarrassed but firm. 'It's just that, for your own protection, I think someone else should be in the room.' She felt a melodramatic heel. This must be some ghastly accident. It was an old building, no doubt the electric wiring had developed a fault. It couldn't be anything else.

She looked round the recently decorated room at the beautifully kept equipment, refused to think of the alternative to a fault in the electrical system but knew she was right to insist on her continuing presence.

'There's got to be something we can do about all this water.' Joel Madoc rose irritably and sloshed his way across to the sink. Before Darina could try and stop him, he opened the cupboard door and started flinging out more tea towels. They sailed on to the floor around the body and collapsed in waterlogged heaps. Knowing protest was useless, Darina went to help, picking up the soaked towels and wringing them out into the bucket Timothy Browne had found. Joel followed her example, gradually working his way towards the door.

Darina looked for more dry towels in the cupboard. The box where they had been kept was empty, she shifted it to see if any more were behind. Then stared unbelievingly at two small crocodile clips securing electric cable to the metal U-bends of the two sinks. She followed the cables back to where they disappeared round the edge of the backless cupboard. Further investigation was blocked by the dishwasher. She looked inside the cupboard again and reckoned the machine was plugged into a socket hidden at the back.

She must have said something because Joel came over, hunkering down beside her to try and see what was causing such concern. At first he didn't understand what Darina was trying to explain. Then he said, 'You mean she was electrocuted by the sink?'

'Those wires are just clipped on to the sink outlets, see, to those bits you unscrew if the sink gets blocked up. The other ends are somewhere behind that dishwasher. No, don't touch anything!' She grabbed Joel's arm as he looked as though he was going to heave the machine out from its place in the run of work cupboards. For a moment his muscles tensed under her

40

restraining grip and it seemed as though he would anyway, then he relaxed.

'Why metal outlets to the sinks, anyway?' Darina asked, grabbing at any excuse to divert his attention from action. 'I thought they all had plastic ones these days.'

'They came from a demolition site. I think Anna organized them when she redid the kitchen, I wasn't part of the company then but I remember a lot of talk about keeping the budget as small as possible.'

They stared at the two round metal sinks let into a white work surface. Both were filled with water. In the first were a couple of small mixing bowls and some utensils. In the second was a stainless-steel saucepan. On the side were a wooden spoon and a plastic spatula, both clean.

Darina looked around at the rest of the working area. The only other item of any significance was a tin filled with what looked at a cursory glance to be a mixture of melted chocolate, broken biscuits, and glacé fruit.

She tried to remember a lecture William had once given her about electricity and its dangers when combined with water. 'It looks,' she said, 'as though someone wired up a positive lead to one sink and a negative to the other. If Marian managed to touch both sinks together, as would have been too easy when moving things from one to another, she would have completed the circuit. With her wet hands she didn't stand a chance.' She looked at him. 'Weren't you using the kitchen before her?'

Joel nodded, staring at the sinks.

'Did you do any washing up?'

He shifted impatiently. 'Of course, the rule is everyone does their own clearing up. Even I don't use the dishwasher, that's reserved for when we entertain.'

'Did you use both bowls?'

He thought briefly. 'Yes. I didn't fill both, though. My practice is to put the dirty stuff in one and wash up in the other. I have the tap running so I can rinse things before leaving them to drain.' A well-trained washer-up.

Darina looked carefully at the sinks, trying to see in her mind's eye the sequence of movements. It seemed highly unlikely that Joel wouldn't also have completed the circuit in some way.

Faintly in the distance she heard an ambulance bell then, more stridently, the siren of a police car rapidly approaching.

Soon responsibility for all of this could be handed over to the law. This was one time, she decided, she was not going to become involved with murder. Then realized with a sinking heart that she already was.

Chapter Six

Anna Drax Johnson drove up to Finer Foods in the late afternoon. The driveway was cluttered with police and other official-looking cars and barred by a white tape slashed with blue. A policeman refused her entry.

'Don't be ridiculous,' she said sharply, the pit of her stomach churning uneasily. 'I work here. What's happened?'

'There's been an accident,' he said with stolid taciturnity.

'Accident! Has someone been hurt? I demand to know what has happened.'

'I'm afraid I can't tell you anything, madam.'

'Take me to your superior officer, I'm a director of this company and entitled to know exactly what is going on.'

The constable spoke into a small radio. After a moment he opened the barrier and waved her through.

It was almost impossible for Anna to find room in the crowded parking area for her BMW but eventually she squeezed it in between a police Ford and the laurel hedge, just managing to open her door wide enough to exit. She scrunched her way through the autumn leaves blown against the hedge and walked quickly up to the front door. There she was met by another uniformed officer who took her into the board room where a number of men were sitting at the table. A heavy-set man with watchful eyes rose to meet her.

'Mrs Drax Johnson?'

'Ms,' she said automatically, glancing around quickly to see if there were any clues as to why they were there. In the hall she had seen only Maggie, working at her word processor with red eyes. The girl had half risen when she'd seen Anna but had been waved back by the constable.

'I'm afraid what I have to tell you will come as rather a shock,' the heavy-set man said courteously. 'Please sit down. I am Chief

Inspector Melville of the CID.' He drew out a chair. Anna carefully lowered herself onto it and heard him ask someone to organize a cup of tea.

Anna Drax Johnson took two deep, slow breaths then said, 'I've been refused entry to my own company, my receptionist has been forbidden to speak to me, and I still haven't been told why.'

'I'm afraid your aunt, Marian Drax, has been electrocuted.'

The shock was completely unexpected. Anna stared at the officer, now sitting on the other side of the table. 'Marian? Electrocuted? There must be some mistake!'

'No mistake, I'm afraid.' He was watching her closely.

'What was she doing? How did it happen?' Anna pushed back the chair and rose clumsily from the table, almost knocking over the cup of tea someone was attempting to place in front of her. 'I must see her, now!' The imperious tone was back in her voice.

'That's impossible, I'm afraid, the body has been taken away.'

'Taken? Where?'

There was a pause. Anna sat down again rather suddenly. The detective was explaining that somehow the sinks in the company kitchen had been wired up, connected to the terminals of the dishwasher plug.

'You mean,' she started slowly, aware his careful eyes were watching her reactions. 'You mean someone deliberately killed my aunt?'

'It seems to look that way,' he replied quietly. Was he really weary or was it just the effect of the deep pouches under those observant eyes?

'But who could have wanted to kill her?'

'That is what we have to find out. You have no idea?'

'Good Heavens, no. She was perfectly harmless, a sweet person.' A wretched financial director, someone hopeless at business, useless at life, but a perfectly sweet person. Who was now dead.

'She was financial director here, I believe?'

'Yes.' Anna looked around her. 'Where's Joel Madoc? Why isn't he here? He's not . . . ?' The question trailed off as she looked at the detective with suddenly darkened eyes.

'Why should you think anything had happened to Mr Madoc?' The question was sharply put.

Anna began to stammer excuses, unable to think straight, painfully conscious that he hadn't confirmed whether Joel was all right or not.

44

At last he ended the suspense. 'Mr Madoc is in his office with a sergeant, giving his statement.' He looked at her then reached across the table and pushed the cup of tea closer to her. 'Drink some, you'll find it helps.'

She picked up the cup automatically and sipped at the hot, sweet liquid.

'Now.' Chief Inspector Melville drew a pad in front of him. 'Can you please tell me where you were this morning?'

'This morning?'

'Yes. I would like a complete timetable from first thing until you arrived here just now.'

Anna stared at him. 'You mean I'm a suspect?'

'Just a matter of routine. We have to know the movements of everyone connected with Miss Drax.'

Of course, this was a police investigation. Everything would be gone into, everyone's motives and opportunities be considered. Well, they would soon find her programme that morning left no unexplained gaps. She put down her cup.

'I got up as usual at six-thirty, did my exercises, had breakfast then drove to the station and caught the eight fifteen to London.'

'Just a minute, which station would this have been?'

Anna told him.

'Right, thank you. So, you caught the train to London. What time did you arrive?'

Anna ran through her agenda in town, giving names and addresses, looking up telephone numbers for him in her personal organizer. 'Then I got the three fifteen train back and drove here straight from the station.'

He asked for her home address then sent her off with a detective sergeant to have the details written down in a formal statement, which she was asked to sign. Finally she was told she could leave. She looked at the police officer, idly noting the strength of his neck as he bent over her statement. 'What will happen now?'

He glanced up at her, dark brown eyes alert. 'Our scene of crime officers are examining the kitchen. Statements are being taken from everyone in the company and we are setting up an Incident Room to co-ordinate the investigation.' He was full of the importance of the occasion.

'When can I see Mr Madoc?'

'I can't say how long his statement will take.' Courteous but uninformative.

Anna went back to the reception hall. Maggie had gone, leaving her desk tidy and the word processor turned off, but the night lines hadn't been switched through. No doubt the police constable who was still there was detailed to answer the phone should it ring.

Before Anna could move towards the Managing Director's office, Michael Berkeley, followed by another policeman, came into the hall, his face drawn and pale, his eyes pits of misery. He went straight to her. 'Anna, have they told you?' She nodded wordlessly then found herself clasped in his arms. She stood awkwardly. 'It's dreadful, unbelievable. I just can't take it in.' He released her and stepped back, his eyes fluttering rapidly as though holding back a Niagara of tears.

'Poor Michael,' she said, feeling tears prick at the back of her eyes for the first time. 'It must be dreadful for you.'

His hand sketched a small, hopeless gesture. 'I think the worst of the shock is over.' The police officer had disappeared into the board room. He glanced at the closed door. 'When I got back, I just couldn't believe it.' His voice broke slightly, he swallowed hard. 'I just couldn't believe it.' His gaze wandered round the reception area, as though Marian might even now emerge from one of the offices and prove the whole nightmare a ghastly mistake. Then he closed his eyes for a moment. 'Let's go and find a drink.'

Anna looked at him more closely. He really was badly shaken and there was an exhausted slouch to his shoulders. 'I thought I'd wait until they'd finished with Joel.'

His face twitched irritably. 'He could be hours yet and I shouldn't think he'd want to see either of us anyway.'

Anna's face assumed the closed expression it wore whenever it seemed she was not going to get her way. But her voice was casual.

'You're probably right. Come back with me, I couldn't stand a pub.'

Michael's car was as badly parked as her own. His hand shook as he got out his keys. Anna closed his fingers over them and said she'd drive him.

Her home was a substantial stone house on the edge of a village some five miles from the company headquarters.

She led the way inside and placed her briefcase by the hall table. The light was flashing on her answering machine. She had forgotten it was Maria's day off, that meant she would have to get her own supper, but at least the bitch had remembered to press the right switch before she left.

Anna ignored the light, hung up her guest's coat, took him through to the living room, and poured out two stiff whiskies.

Michael collapsed on to a sofa and took a deep swig. Then he put the glass down on to a large coffee table and sat with his head in his hands.

Anna sank back into an armchair and sipped at her drink. The glass knocked against her teeth and her hand was shaking. Carefully she lowered the drink.

After a moment she said, 'I'm terribly sorry, Michael, I know how fond of her you were.'

'Fond!' he said savagely and raised his head. 'You know, she had only to say the word and I'd've left Ellen, no matter what.'

'I don't think she wanted that kind of responsibility,' Anna said after a pause.

Michael's second gulp of whisky nearly drained the glass. 'You know there was only one person she was really interested in. I never stood much of a chance. And what had I to offer her anyway? There wouldn't have been much money, Ellen would have seen to that. As you know, my attempts to improve things aren't always gloriously successful. That's why . . .' He didn't finish the sentence.

Anna shifted her position in the chair. 'Money didn't matter to Marian, not really. She was genuinely fond of you, Michael, I know she was.' She forced herself to continue. 'After Joel married Jane Leslie, she could easily have turned to you.'

The Sales Director raised his head. 'You know how much that news upset her?'

'Oh yes!' Anna took Michael's empty glass and refilled it. 'I was there when she heard it; she didn't take it at all well. In fact she said something about stopping the match.' She gave him a swift glance. 'I can't imagine how, you only have to look at those two to see they can hardly keep their hands off each other. And she should certainly have seen it coming, for the last few months that woman has positively haunted our offices.'

She replaced the whisky decanter on the drinks table carefully, barely containing her fear and anger, and gave Michael the recharged glass.

Michael was managing to look even more miserable. 'When Eleanor was dying, Marian hinted to me she would be taking her place. After a decent interval.'

Once that knowledge had nearly destroyed Anna. 'That can't be true!' she said. Even now she found she could not afford to admit what she knew.

Something in her voice caused Michael to drag himself out of his self-absorption. 'Maybe not,' he acknowledged after a moment. 'Perhaps I just misunderstood things. I misunderstand such a lot.'

She shied away from his self-pity, refilled her own glass then moved to draw the curtains against the dark that now pressed against the windows, tugging at the material with furious energy.

Michael raised his head as rings clashed against the wooden rods. 'What are we going to do?'

'What do you mean?' Anna threw herself back into her chair, spilling some of her whisky, then raised the glass and drank, relishing the smoky malt firing its way down her throat, relieved to find her body had not blotted out all sensation.

'Well, our plans . . . for the company?' He couldn't bring himself to spell it out.

'We continue as before,' Anna said softly. She was in control again now.

'But without Marian . . .'

'I don't see that it will make any difference, not in the long run.'

'There will have to be a new financial director,' he pointed out.

'That could be an advantage. At least the accounting will be properly done. What matters is the future, not the past.'

'But what if the past haunts us?'

'There is nothing that can haunt us.' Anna was briskly matter-of-fact. 'Everything has been organized and will continue exactly as we planned. Whatever happens, whether Joel goes or stays, we shall be winners.'

She devoted the next hour to explaining to Michael once again exactly why they didn't have to worry.

Then she ordered a taxi, helped him in, and waved him off, then went back inside and closed the front door. Once the heavy wood had clunked shut, she leant against its weight and allowed weariness at last to soak into her bones. What a mess everything was.

The telephone rang and the light on her answering machine flashed. Anna forced herself to take the few steps necessary to pick up the phone before the tape could take over.

Chapter Seven

William listened incredulously as Darina gave him the details of her disastrous morning at Finer Foods.

'What is it about you?' he asked as they sat eating supper. 'Are you some sort of lightning conductor for murder? Everywhere you go dead bodies appear. Now, I suppose, you're going to get busy trying to solve the case.'

'Not this one,' asserted his fiancé. 'It's nothing to do with me, nor, thank Heavens, you.'

'I feel like ringing Wiltshire police and warning them.'

'I promise I'm not going to do any detecting.'

'Nothing has stopped you in the past.'

'But I was involved then, I'm not here.' Even to herself her voice sounded unconvincing.

'I can't see much difference. You were on the scene when the body was found. You've met the murdered woman, got to know something about her colleagues. You're not going to tell me you haven't been wondering why she was murdered and by whom?'

Darina looked at him carefully. Was he teasing or really upset? He gave her a mischievous smile and she relaxed. She had meant it, she had no intention of involving herself in this case. All the same, it did raise interesting questions.

'That trap was quite carefully laid,' she said tentatively, giving her fiancé another quick glance. He merely poured more wine into their glasses. 'And it had to have been sprung between the time Joel Madoc finished his session and Marian Drax started hers.' She explained about the washing up.

William got up from the table and went over to the sink. 'Show me, will you?' Darina followed, amused at the speed with which his own curiosity had been aroused.

She piled the dirty pots and pans from their supper into one half of the double sink and filled the other with water. 'Now, this

49

is more or less how Joel told me he did his clearing up. Of course, the set-up is slightly different because the Finer Foods' sinks are separate, it wouldn't work with one like this because you couldn't keep the positive apart from the negative.'

William grinned at her. 'So you really were listening when I gave that little lecture?'

'Don't I always? Look,' she said, moving saucepans from one sink to the other, cleaning and rinsing, 'I don't think it's possible not to complete the circuit in some way.'

William took her place and experimented. 'Hmm,' he said after a bit. 'With extraordinary care, I suppose it just might be, but that would presuppose Joel Madoc was aware of the situation or was an extraordinarily careful person. Is he?'

Darina thought about the contradictory aspects of the Finer Foods managing director. 'Controlled, yes; careful, I don't think so.'

'So the circuit had to be set up after his session had finished. How easy would it have been to fix?'

'I've been thinking about that. Don't give me that look, you're just as interested.'

'Don't fool yourself, I'm treating it as a pleasant mental exercise to distract my thoughts from the wretched cases I've got on my desk.'

This was the first time they had been together for any length of time for several days. William had been leaving first thing each morning and coming back after supper, falling into bed too tired for more than a few words about the day.

Not certain this was the best use of such precious time but unable to resist delving further into the complexities surrounding Marian Drax's death, Darina outlined how the sinks had been electrified.

'So you couldn't see how the wires were connected to the electricity supply?' William started to help clear up.

'It looked as though they probably went to the back of the dishwasher.'

'Sounds an arrangement that would have taken time to set up.'

'Right. But it needn't have taken any time to fix the crocodile clips on to the U-bends, when I saw them they were just fastened to the lip round the junction screw. The wires could have been set up except for the final bit of clipping on then tucked behind one of the boxes in the cupboard, there was one containing tea towels and another filled with cleaning bits and pieces. Perhaps one was put behind each, to make sure they didn't accidentally touch if anybody fiddled about in there. They would have been quite unnoticeable to anyone casually opening the door.'

'So all it would have needed for the final bit of electrification was a quick opening of the cupboard and fixing of the clips?'

'Right! Someone could have darted in and done it in seconds, leaving it all set up for the next user of the kitchen.'

'Who was Marian Drax. This sounds much easier than any of my cases. Who knew she was going to be in there at that time?'

'There's a company notice board in the corner of the reception hall, everyone passes it coming in or going out whether they work in the extension or in the old part of the offices. It holds details of the sports club, offers of damaged stock, items members of the staff want to buy and sell, that sort of thing, plus a roster for the kitchen. People fill in their names for particular sessions. The competition's proving very popular and there are very few blank spaces. I checked the board this afternoon, just before the police removed it.'

'And who said she definitely wasn't going to be involved in any investigating?'

'Don't look at me like that. You admitted yourself I had to have a certain interest. If you're not careful, I shan't tell you any more.' William shot her an amused look and topped up her glass of wine. 'Anyway, there was a roster for three weeks up there. This is the last week of the competition and every space had been filled. Marian Drax had her name down twice, once for Monday and once for today, Thursday, just after Joel Madoc's session.'

'So anyone in the company would have known she would be using the kitchen at that time and could have set up the wires, perhaps during a session of their own, then triggered it off just before she was due in there. Which brings us to the next question; how easy would it be to slip into the kitchen?'

Darina frowned. 'Maggie, that's the receptionist, has a desk in clear sight of the doors to the kitchen, board room, and Joel's office. She can see anyone going into any of those rooms.'

'Could she have been called away for any reason?'

'I should think so. She showed a chap into the board room while I was there, just before the power blinked. But I don't think,' she added as William started to speak, 'that that's when the murderer could have got into the kitchen. Apart from him or her having to emerge again, Marian Drax must have gone in there some time before.'

'Well, no doubt the police in charge of the investigation will sort that one out quite easily.'

Darina placed coffee on a tray with a couple of mugs and they went into the living room. She shivered. 'The weather's getting quite cold, what happened to those Indian summers we used to get in October?'

William bent and applied a match to the fire already laid in their wood-burning stove. 'What about motive? Have you identified any suspects?'

Darina watched as flames licked the kindling behind the glass doors. 'I keep remembering how upset Marian Drax seemed to be when Joel announced his engagement. She said she'd make sure they never married.'

'How was she going to do that?'

'She broke down at that point and left the room. Joel made it into some sort of joke but there was a moment he looked . . .' She paused, remembering the frozen group of people in the kitchen after Marian's departure. The image of a jungle cat gliding through the undergrowth slipped into her mind. 'There was something feral about him.'

William smiled. 'Did you tell the police that?'

'About Marian's comment, yes. But repeated, it sounded like the sort of hysterical threat people make when they don't know what else to say.'

'She was the company accountant, wasn't she? Perhaps personal emotions had nothing to do with her death. You say the company is in some financial difficulty, what if she had uncovered a fraud of some sort?'

'I don't think she would know what fraud was if it spelt itself out.' Darina thought back to that introductory lunch. 'She's been refusing to computerize the company accounts. From something Michael Berkeley, the sales director, said, I think she's more of a book-keeper than an accountant.'

'I thought every company was computerized these days! Why was she hesitating, could she have been afraid of some dodgy accounting of her own coming to light?'

Darina thought about the faded woman who had seemed so ineffectual and so deeply unhappy. 'Again, I would doubt she had either the skill or the guts to carry out something like that. And even if she had it would hardly have got her killed. No, I think she honestly couldn't cope with the problems of getting to grips with the computer age, she seemed terrified of being proved incompetent.'

'Sounds as though she probably was. How on earth did she come to be in that position?'

'It was her father who built up the firm. I should think she's a major shareholder.'

'Interesting to know who gets her shares now, in that case. Have you any idea who will benefit from her death? Has she any family?'

'Not so far as I know, I think she was unmarried, though the fact she called herself Drax needn't mean anything. Her sister retained the family name through two marriages and Anna is known as Drax Johnson. But Marian had the air of a certain sort of spinster, that slightly self-absorbed, fine-drawn aura of someone who has no one to think about but herself.'

'If there is a power struggle going on in the firm, her shares could be valuable.'

'Joel said during that lunch that he had a majority.'

'Did he mean just more than anybody else or more than fifty per cent?'

'You mean if he had anything less than that, he could be out-voted if the other shareholders got together?' Once again Darina considered the lunchtime confrontation. Anna versus Joel it had boiled down to. With Marian appearing to support her niece. Where exactly had Peter Drax stood? He wasn't too happy over the financial situation but it hadn't been clear where his support would be placed should it come to showdown time. And would Marian Drax really have voted against Joel? That confrontation in the kitchen had suggested an emotional involvement. Had Joel been two-timing his wife or Jane Leslie, or both? Did he have his father's attitude to monogamy? What was it he had said, impossible to ask a bull to keep to one heifer?

'It might just have been, of course, that someone was jealous of her recipe and wanted the trip to Hong Kong.'

A cushion flung with force but no accuracy narrowly missed William's coffee cup. 'I told you,' his fiancée declared, 'I have no intention of playing detective in the case of Marian Drax. Let's talk about something else.'

Chapter Eight

Jane Leslie reached up on tiptoe to take out the casserole from Joel Madoc's oven. When they were married she was going to have to do something about this oven. She was going to have to do something about the house as well, maybe suggest they lived somewhere else. But she couldn't think about that now. Now she had to get them through each day as it came. It didn't leave her energy for anything else.

'Everything ready?' Joel stood in the kitchen doorway.

Before Thursday (everything in Jane's mind was now labelled Before or After Thursday), he would have come and put his arms around her, kissed the nape of her neck just below her hair, teased her into wriggling free with a protest that there was a time for everything and now wasn't the time for that. But this evening he just stood there, one hand in his pocket jingling change, the other flipping a thumb across his fingers again and again, a nervous gesture that set Jane's teeth on edge. What she wanted to do was force him to look at her, look at her properly, and see that he was not the only one being made miserable by the ghastly blow fate had dealt them.

What she did was to nod briefly, her gaze automatically checking the table laid for four. The meal was to be in the kitchen but with the Georg Jensen silver, the Baccarat crystal, and crisp linen napkins, informality mixed with style, she hoped it was going to prove a winning combination.

She turned her attention to the casserole, unable to stand the worried look in Joel's eyes. She wanted him to be strong, decisive, in control. 'The meat's nearly ready, when did you say they were coming?'

'Any moment now.'

It was Sunday evening. To say the previous few days had been difficult was like saying it was a long way to China or that cattle didn't like going to slaughter. And there seemed little hope the coming days would be any easier. 'Do you really think they can help?'

'I can't think of anyone else who might be able to.'

Joel's solicitor had been no help at all. Legal niceties seemed all he was able to offer. Still, it was thanks to him Joel was here to share this meal, that Joel wasn't . . . but Jane wasn't going to think about that.

Any more than she was going to think about what this investigation into Marian Drax's death could dredge up.

Joel raised his head. 'I can hear a car.' He was at the front door in a moment. Jane removed her apron and followed more slowly.

Standing on the doorstep was Darina Lisle. But no detective inspector fiancé appeared to be with her.

'I'm sorry,' she apologized, 'William couldn't make it. He's got so much on his plate with this promotion. He sends his apologies.'

Jane watched Joel's shoulders sag slightly and cursed the absent detective inspector. She doubted the validity of the excuse; he wanted to protect his position, more likely, not get involved in another police force's case. People were like that, helping someone out never came into it if it would put their own position in danger. Then she forced a smile as Darina greeted her.

The tall girl – Jane thought the oven would offer no problem to her – gave Joel her jacket then looked around in astonishment. 'What an amazing house!'

Jane remembered her own first visit. How the startling angles and expanses of glass had taken her breath away. The double height of the living area that encompassed hall, sitting, and dining spaces had seemed to soar up for ever, like a cathedral. An open-tread staircase winging its way up to a second floor that only covered half the house's floor space seemed dangerously unprotected. It was all so stark, so modern. Minimal furniture, minimal wall space, nowhere to hang pictures, place cabinets, display bits and bobs, and always the huge windows. It was like living in a box made of glass. At least there was no one to see in, buried as it was in the woods. Jane always insisted on turning on all the lights so that golden splashes lit the garden, driving away shadows from the encroaching trees. No curtains to draw against the night, only blinds to provide protection from the sun. Yes, the house would definitely have to go.

Joel poured drinks; Darina asked for a white wine spritzer, explaining she had to drive home.

Jane should be driving home herself. Staying here with Joel meant she had to leave too early in the morning, there was so much to do before the delicatessen opened, but she couldn't leave him, not in such a state.

She put Italian bread under the grill for olive and anchovy bruschetta to eat with the drinks. When she returned to the living area Joel had broached the heart of the matter.

'The police believe I killed Marian,' he was saying. He stopped pacing the polished wood floor and sat heavily in his Charles Eames chair.

Darina Lisle accepted a wedge of the fragrant bread and sipped her mixture of white wine and sparkling mineral water. She was sitting on the leather sofa, her long fair hair piled on top of her head, her body beautifully relaxed. The sight did nothing to soothe Jane's jangled nerve ends. 'Have they told you so?' their guest asked.

'They don't have to in so many words. They interrogated me all Thursday afternoon and into the evening. And on Friday they asked me to go down to the police station for more interrogation and everything was recorded.'

'He was kept in overnight, imprisoned,' said Jane, sitting in the other Charles Eames chair beside Joel and reaching out for his hand. Goose bumps came up on her neck and arms as she thought of him in one of those stark cells that robbed you of all dignity.

'In custody is what I think they call it,' Joel said with a grimace. 'But by Saturday, yesterday, my God it seems longer ago than that, my solicitor managed to get me out.'

'The police aren't allowed to keep you more than twenty-four hours without charging you,' said Darina slowly. 'If they didn't do that, it sounds as though they aren't sure of their case. Exactly why do they suspect you?'

Joel leaned forward. 'They say I must have electrified the sink. Maggie apparently didn't see anyone go into the kitchen during the few minutes between the time I finished my session and Marian started hers. She swears, according to the police, that she was at her desk the whole time and nobody could have gone in without her noticing them. Ergo, they say, I must have activated that electric connection.'

'In other words, you are the person with the opportunity. But what about motive, have they suggested what that could be?'

56

'They keep harking on about our arguments over the accountancy arrangements. As if I'd kill someone so that a computer could be brought in! Or that I couldn't have got rid of her some other way.'

'And that's their only suggestion?'

Joel picked up his drink. Before he'd appeared outraged, humiliated, depressed. Now he seemed uncomfortable and Jane saw his eyes shift in her direction. She hadn't thought before to ask why he could have wanted to kill the Financial Director, it hadn't seemed relevant. Now she remembered Marian's little outburst when Joel had announced their engagement. What, exactly, had she meant? Joel hadn't wanted to discuss it, told her to dismiss the silly woman from her mind. Was it possible . . . suddenly Jane felt like a novice skier at the top of a terrifying slope.

'It's all they've produced so far,' Joel said, mumbling into his glass.

'Is there another motive they could discover?' pressed Darina, her eyes watchful. Jane could see them noting the way Joel rearranged his weight in the chair, avoided looking at either of them.

'No,' he said after the briefest of pauses. 'No, I can't think of any reason.'

Darina ran a finger round the rim of her glass, contemplating its pale gold contents, then looked straight at Joel. 'Why exactly did you ask William and me here?'

Joel returned her look, appeal in his brown eyes. 'Charles told me you'd solved other murders and I hoped that, maybe with the help of your fiancé, you might be able to sort this one out. Clear my name.'

The tall girl shook her head regretfully. 'I'm afraid I'm not a proper detective, I was just lucky with those other deaths. And it would be quite improper for William to become involved in someone else's case, even if he had the time.' Just as Jane had thought, she knew a moment's pleasure at being proved right, even though she couldn't broadcast the fact.

Darina's grey eyes were concerned. 'I can understand what you are going through at the moment, but I have great confidence in the ability of the police to get to the bottom of things.'

Jane felt renewed despair. She hadn't believed anything would come of this evening but there had been a faint chance that such a maverick approach might have got them somewhere. Might have meant the police wouldn't have to dig too deeply into all their affairs.

'Do say you'll try to help,' she pleaded. 'We're desperate!' She made her tone as soft and compelling as she could. But she knew that it never had the effect on women that it did on men. On Joel, for instance.

As if it was yesterday, Jane could see him standing in her delicatessen store room, looking up at her as she balanced precariously on a chair and tried to reach a box of cocktail snacks from the top shelf. She didn't know what a stranger was doing wandering into the back reaches of her shop but he had appeared at exactly the right moment.

He'd placed both hands round her waist and gently helped her down from the chair, then climbed on it himself and lifted the box off the shelf. 'Never let me see you doing that again,' he'd said. She'd murmured something about broken steps, looked into his brown eyes, and it was as if some sort of current had been switched on. Feelings she thought she'd managed to bury so deep no man could stir them again twitched infinitesimally with tiny movements, like those of some almost invisible filaments. She had ignored the stirring but found herself offering him a cup of coffee and then listening to how he'd joined Finer Foods to help his wife, Eleanor Drax. It was the first time Jane had heard she was unwell.

The dynamic head of Finer Foods had been most helpful when Jane had first bought the delicatessen, then so rundown that the specialist company had not thought it worthy of their products. But Jane knew, if she was to have the sort of shop she wanted, it had to stock Finer Foods' goods. So she'd approached them and had an interview with Eleanor Drax.

She remembered a tall, elegant woman who had shown no impatience at the number of questions Jane had asked, had been generous with her advice and, at the end, given her a tour of the warehouse. She had left the company clutching a notebook filled with suggestions. Mrs Drax had struck her as shrewd, practical, and dedicated to the business she ran.

A few months later she had asked Eleanor Drax over, shown her the revamped shop, the new layout, the chilled cabinet and freezer section with their brand-new equipment, her computerized cash registers, the smartly rebuilt display windows with their old-fashioned gold lettering that reeked of quality and style. Approval was graciously given and Jane had been able to place her first order. Several months later Mrs Drax had popped in without notice, said she had found herself in the neighbourhood and wanted to see how Jane Leslie was getting on. But she must have known from the orders that business was good. Jane reckoned she just wanted to find out if she was managing to keep up her standards of cleanliness and display.

Jane wondered what Eleanor Drax was like to live with. She had seemed some years older than her husband but she was an attractive and stylish woman; was that enough to hold this man? This man who could so quickly stimulate a sexual response?

Jane had expressed regret at Mrs Drax's illness but all she could really take in was the look in Joel Madoc's eyes as he told her he was trying to learn the business as fast as he could. He was going round the region, visiting major outlets. Was hers a major outlet, she asked?

He'd been told it was one of the best in the south of England, if not the whole country, and if she had time to show him around, guide him through which products sold and why, he'd be eternally grateful.

He had spent the rest of the day in the delicatessen, exploring along the shelves, listening to her difficulties with delivery systems and taking her through the principles she had evolved for selecting new products.

At first she thought he was spending so much time in the delicatessen to impress her and kept her answers to his queries short and factual. Gradually she realized he was deadly serious. He really did want to know everything about the trade and how the Finer Foods products were doing. And gradually she began to believe she had misread the look in his eyes. Which was probably just as well. She had built up a good business here and had no intention of jeopardizing it. So she'd not relaxed her manner and had been quite brief with him at the end of the day when he'd thanked her for all her time, polite but brief. She was sure then there was no chance he could slip under her guard. Almost, though, she had expected him to return a few days later, or to ring her, perhaps ask her out to lunch. But he hadn't.

Not until after Eleanor Drax had been buried. She'd died two months after Joel Madoc's visit. Jane hadn't gone to the funeral, she hadn't felt it was her place.

A few days later, just after five in the afternoon, Joel Madoc returned to the delicatessen. A late customer was keeping Jane's assistant busy, asking for first one thing and then another. Jane quietly cleared up in the background. She had been about to lock the entrance door when she'd seen him through the glass. He'd cocked his head and raised an eyebrow as he realized the shop was shutting. She'd opened the door, of course, unable to stop a warm smile illuminating her face.

Behind her she could hear the customer apologizing for keeping them open. 'If I'd realized you closed at five o'clock, I'd have finished ages ago.'

'We're delighted to have been of help,' Jane said as Joel stood on one side to let the customer leave. She told her assistant not to worry about the rest of the clearing up, she'd look after that. The girl had thrown an interested look in Joel's direction but obediently took off her apron and left.

Condolences for Eleanor's death had been dismissed. 'Please, let's take all that as read. It was a hellish path she had to travel and at last she's at rest. I don't want to think about that any more.'

No, Jane learned over the next few months, Joel never wanted to think about the sad and awkward things of life. He put all his energies into creating new horizons, building new castles. When he was brought face to face with unpalatable situations, ones that proved intractable to his charm and drive, he preferred to turn his back rather than seek other ways of dealing with them.

So now it was doubly difficult for him to be faced with the awful fact of Marian Drax's death.

She heard Darina Lisle once again refuse to become involved in any investigation. 'Let's eat,' Jane said. Food, she believed, always helped awkward situations. As they fed the inner man, people relaxed, let down their defences. No wonder so much business was done over the luncheon table.

Over the supper table, Jane asked Darina how her research was coming along. From Finer Foods' products they progressed quite naturally to discussing the company.

'Just how deep is the financial trouble?' their guest asked.

Joel helped himself to more of the gratin dauphinois. 'That's the difficulty. I don't really know. After Eleanor's death our income started dipping, quite sharply, but the reasons for it could lie much further back. Marian couldn't or wouldn't produce the information I need. We could be heading for bankruptcy and I would have no idea. She's never made proper provision for amortizing capital investment, re-assessing company assets, or any other regular accountancy procedures, as far as I can see. And she's never understood costing principles. If only Eleanor had let me take a hand much earlier. She was a brilliant saleswoman and very shrewd in many ways but financially she was as innocent as her sister.

'As far as Marian is concerned, as long as the turnover keeps going up, she thinks we are all right. I can't, couldn't,' he corrected himself quickly, 'get it through to her that there is more to running a successful business than turnover. The fact that we shall have to reduce the current dividend should have told her, it certainly got through to Peter, as that directors' lunch showed. I'm sorry I put you through that, by the way, but I thought you should know exactly what I was up against. And I had to convince Marian that unless she took the necessary steps to modernize her procedures, she would lose her job. In fact, I think she would have lost it anyway, she just wasn't up to providing the financial service a company like ours must have.'

'From what you've told me, it's been beyond her for years,' Jane heard herself saying. 'I don't mean to sound unpleasant, particularly now Marian is dead, but if Eleanor hadn't been so ill, wouldn't she have sorted out her sister?'

'She had mentioned it,' Joel admitted. 'But she really wasn't well enough to cope. It was one of the reasons she brought me in.'

'If it's not your sales, have you any idea where the trouble does lie?' asked Darina.

'There's a large section of cash business that's done with Chinese restaurants. Talk about not using computers, I think most of them rely on an abacus and feel a written invoice carries the evil eye.'

'More likely they know the Inland Revenue have difficulty pinning down profits when they've only got the minimum recorded in black and white,' commented Jane drily.

'So you think some of the cash has been, as you might say, liberated before it reaches you? What about the sales department, don't they know exactly how much has been sold and what should be received?'

'You'd think so,' said Joel. 'Yet I have had a lot of trouble trying to pin Michael down on this. It's all talk of special prices, bulk orders, split orders, any sort of orders. It's almost as though he was in league with Marian.'

'Well, you told me yourself he's been dotty about her for years.' Jane cleared away the plates and served a mango creamed ice.

'From one of our tins?' asked Joel as she passed the glass bowl around.

'Of course.' Jane was proud of her headily aromatic dessert, no one ever believed it didn't contain any cream; but Darina appeared oblivious of its charms, she was looking intently at Joel. 'You really feel Michael and Marian might have been in cahoots?'

He held the bowl and stared at her. 'Cahoots? Yes, that's it! You've put your finger on it, I knew you'd help. Look,' he continued rapidly. 'Let's suppose, nothing more, just suppose that Michael has been skimming off cash from the Chinese restaurant business, either starting as Eleanor died or perhaps becoming more greedy then. And let's suppose Marian knew. Well, it was likely she would, wasn't it? She'd see the returns from each restaurant, even with her Mickey Mouse system. Here I come along, insisting we put everything on computer, be able to compare figures, extrapolate trends, well, she would think it was all going to come out.'

'You mean she was trying to protect Michael?' Jane asked, trying to follow his line of reasoning.

'Trying to protect herself! Because she would be on the line just as much as him. Perhaps she went to him and said it wouldn't be possible to keep quiet about it any longer.'

'Could she have been taking a share?' Jane felt quite excited. For the first time since the accident, Joel was sounding cheerful and constructive.

'Perhaps that's it. Marian goes to Michael and, whether she's sharing in the scam or not, he knows that he has to protect himself and kills her!' There was silence round the table as Joel finished.

'Well?' he said to Darina. 'Don't you think that's what must have happened?'

Chapter Nine

Joel seemed reborn, a man who once again had something to live for.

Darina felt it a pity to puncture his theory, but had to ask, 'How did Michael electrify the sink? I understood he was out all day Thursday, visiting Chinese restaurants in London.'

'It was obviously an alibi. He must have slipped back.'

'If there is a hole in his story, I am sure the police will find it.'

'The police! He will have got some Chinese chap to lie for him! I bet he's got a number of them in his pocket, probably lets them have some tins of abalone cheap and claims it's been stolen from his boot. Wouldn't be the first time something like that's happened.'

'Is abalone expensive?' Darina was diverted for a moment, always interested in unusual ingredients.

'Very! It's a mark of prestige in Chinese entertaining, always given to an important guest. Abalone acknowledges his status.'

'Do you really think he could persuade a Chinaman to lie for him? In my experience they are basically a very honest and truthful race.'

Joel turned to Jane Leslie in some surprise. 'I didn't know you were acquainted with the Chinese!'

Colour flushed Jane's round face. 'My husband was in the Army and we were stationed in Hong Kong. I got very interested in China, we were there when it started opening up, and, of course, we had Chinese servants.'

'You never told me anything about this,' said Joel, almost accusingly, Darina thought.

The flush faded and Jane's face was as pale as milk. 'It's never come up,' she said quickly. 'You know it wasn't a particularly happy episode of my life.'

Joel put a hand over hers. 'I'm sorry, sweet, I didn't mean to upset you. That's where you learned so much about Chinese food, I suppose?'

Jane nodded then suggested they take coffee through to the living area.

Darina made a mental note to have a word with Jane about Chinese cooking as she settled down on the leather sofa and accepted a cup of excellent coffee. Then she got back to the matter on hand. 'You think Michael could have got enough Chinese restaurateurs to swear a false alibi for him? There would be several hours to account for,' she warned.

'He must have done,' Joel stated with conviction.

Darina turned to the next difficulty. 'How do you think he got into the kitchen unobserved?'

Joel played with an executive toy, sending metal balls clicking and swinging back and forth. 'There must be some way. I bet Maggie wasn't keeping as good an eye on the kitchen door as she swears. Michael melts into the background rather easily, don't you think? He's not the sort of fellow you actually notice, is he?'

Joel might have something there, Darina thought. Wasn't there a detective story where a receptionist swore no one came into the office at a certain time, completely ignoring the fact that the postman had because she didn't count him as a person? But she didn't see Michael as quite such an anonymous personality as Joel was trying to suggest. Could there, she wondered, be some undisclosed jealousy here? It seemed unlikely that a man with so much personality as Joel could be jealous of quiet Michael Berkeley, even with his good looks, but she filed away the thought.

'What about the cleaners?' she asked. 'Do they pop into the kitchen from time to time?'

'Only early in the morning when the rest of the offices are done. That's why we insist everyone has to clear up properly after themselves.'

'No chance that someone looking like a cleaner could have gone into the kitchen? Perhaps Maggie wouldn't have noticed them.'

'Now, there's an idea! But I don't see Michael dressing up as a cleaner!' Quite obviously, nothing was going to divert him from his conviction that the Sales Director was the murderer.

Darina tried a different approach. 'What about the financial situation? Who can you get to search for discrepancies in the Chinese restaurant accounts?'

Joel sighed. 'Marian kept everything so closely under her

control the only other people in the department are a couple of clerks and all they are fit for is entering cheques and typing out invoices. I shall have to find someone qualified and pretty damn quickly too. Something else to get on to in the morning.'

Darina thought, but didn't say, that if the police hadn't already impounded the books they would be doing so very shortly, and examining them with the care of a high school teacher searching for nits. Motive for the murder of a financial director could well be found in the company accounts. If Michael Berkeley had been skimming off the cash payments in some way, they would probably discover it. She went back to other possibilities surrounding the fatal morning.

'Are you sure you would have completed the circuit while you were washing up? That is, if the wires had been connected?' she asked Joel.

He grimaced, an expression that combined incredulity with impatience. 'The police took me through every movement I made and there is, I'm afraid, no doubt.'

Surely, if he was guilty, he'd never demonstrate so conclusively how the current could not have been connected until after he'd finished his session? He must realize exactly what that meant?

Jane refilled the empty coffee cups and Darina watched her, wondering what had gone wrong with her marriage. She seemed such a pliant person, able to bend beneath most demands, a first-class candidate for the perfect wife. Look at the way Joel responded to her soothing manner, he'd given up the nervous way he had been fiddling with his executive toy and now sat back in his chair. It must have been something to do with the husband. Had he been a womanizer? It might be an idea to get to know Jane Leslie a little better. Darina asked if she might visit her delicatessen.

The request appeared to be greeted with delight. 'Of course, why don't you come over next Friday, the shop's full of people then and you can talk to some of my regular customers, find out what they are looking for, what they think of the Finer Foods products.'

'But isn't that a very busy day for you?'

'I have lots of assistants at the weekend and after lunch there won't be any reps calling, they're the ones who keep interrupting me!' She glanced teasingly at Joel. 'I sometimes think how much easier it would be to run things if they didn't keep calling!'

Darina grinned at her. 'I've heard hoteliers say how marvellous running a hotel would be if it weren't for the staff and the guests; much the same problem, I suppose?'

'But I would never not want my customers, I love talking to them.'

'Don't they bring you problems?'

'Only when something's wrong and then I want to know so I can put things right. Or sometimes they want something I don't stock. And that's interesting because then I have to try and hunt it down and see if it's worth ordering. People think if they ask for something once it demonstrates a demand and expect to see the product on my shelves the following week. But I might have to buy twenty-four and only sell one.'

They made a date for the following Friday then Darina said it was getting late and she must get home.

Joel held her hand as he said goodbye. 'I can't tell you how grateful I am that you came over. Our chat has cleared things in my mind and I'm going to tackle Michael in the morning.'

'Do you think that's wise?'

'Yes, darling,' Jane Leslie rushed in. 'Think, if he's guilty you'll only ring alarm bells and if he's innocent you could upset him. He might resign!'

Joel laughed. 'Michael Berkeley resign? Where would he get another job at his age? He likes his life style far too much to risk unemployment. And what could I alert him to? No, I shall definitely have a chat with him.' He looked down into Jane's face and used his thumb to smooth away the lines etched into her forehead. 'Don't worry so, I won't be rash. Tell you what, why don't I have Darina present, she can make sure I don't get into trouble?'

Darina disapproved of the whole enterprise, it was amateurish and unlikely to prove productive. On the other hand, Michael Berkeley's reaction to any challenges of his doings on Thursday could be interesting. Maybe something helpful could come of it.

'All right,' she said, 'I was going to come into the office tomorrow anyway.'

William was in bed when she got home, the duvet covered with papers. As she came in, he took off the glasses he'd recently taken to using for reading. 'How did it go?'

She made them a nightcap then told him all about the evening as she got undressed.

66

'I seem to be being dragged into this investigation whether I like it or not. Joel won't be deflected from talking to Michael Berkeley and it seems better to be there, don't you think?' she added doubtfully.

'I think wild horses wouldn't keep you from being present at any such confrontation. I knew you couldn't resist becoming involved in some way.'

'It's just this interview,' Darina assured him.

He gave her a most old-fashioned look and waved a foot, sticking it out from under the duvet. 'Want to hear a pretty little chime?'

'You keep your bells, and your legs, to yourself! No, don't!' she yelled as, regardless of his papers, he dragged her on to the bed.

Chapter Ten

Michael Berkeley woke late on Monday morning.

He opened his eyes and groaned as the bright sun hit his aching retinas. So much for trying to escape reality in whisky. On the bedside table sat a cup of cold tea, placed there by his wife before she'd left for work. He wished she had shaken him properly awake but that would have violated their code.

Slowly he levered himself up in the bed, wincing as his body protested. Just what had he been up to the previous night? He glanced over at the chest of drawers where he always emptied his pockets before taking off his suit. There, in the ashtray that he used for small change, he could see the ends of two gambling chips. He closed his eyes hoping it had been an illusion, that was the last thing he could afford at the moment, in any sense.

He groped for the cup and gulped cold tea; any liquid was welcome in his state. He wondered why Ellen still bothered with it when most of the time it was left untouched. No doubt it was part of the charade she maintained that they were still a happily married couple.

To be fair, she had given him his opportunity. He remembered her sitting in one of the damask-covered chairs that matched the sofa in their lounge, her legs that would have graced the grandest of pianos neatly slanted to one side, hands clasped loosely in her lap. 'I won't interfere with your life,' she'd said. 'The children are grown up, you are free to leave if that is what you want.' A look of obstinate martyrdom had come over her stubbornly plain face. 'I won't remind you of all I've done to make life as comfortable as possible, all the sacrifices I've made so you could do what you wanted.'

And what sacrifices were they, he'd almost asked? What had she really wanted that she hadn't had? He'd been a good provider, a good father. All right, so maybe he hadn't always managed to get round to those little jobs she wanted done around the house and maybe he hadn't always turned up on those school occasions when dads were supposed to be there, shouting on the touchline, clapping at prize day, chatting to teachers when it was parents' evening. But the boys had done all right just the same.

Adrian had nearly completed his accountancy exams and Mark was doing well in banking. Of course, banking was more precarious a profession these days than it had been but Mark would be all right. Both boys were like that. They conformed, harnessed their bright brains to the secure ways of life. In a few years they would be married to suitable girls, have manageable mortgages on solid suburban houses, no doubt have started raising their own ideal families. They were launched on life.

Michael leant against his pillows, pain sawing away just above his eyebrows, trying to allay the itch in his teeth with the cold tea, and wondered just why he hadn't left home as he'd sworn to himself he would once the boys were off his hands.

Had it been Ellen? He'd known when she sat in that chair and loosed the invisible chains that had held him, known with an awful certainty that, despite the way she filled her days, her receptionist's job at the dentist's, her secretaryship of the local Women's Institute, her French evening classes, that she relied on having him for weekends even if she saw him no more than the odd night during the week. Without him at least half there she would lose her status. In Ellen's circle, an absent husband who was director of a well-known food firm was an asset and to be a divorcé definitely a liability.

And she did make him comfortable. She ironed his shirts, saw he was well fed, on the few occasions he dined at home, kept that home neat and tidy.

He knew, though, that it was the financial angle that had kept him prisoner in this wall-to-wall carpeted life style. If he had to divide his reasonably generous income in two, there would be no spare cash for gambling, his dreams of making a fortune or even of retrieving what he had lost at the table would dissolve. He wouldn't be able to afford his smart clothes, Italian shoes, meals in expensive restaurants.

He was sure Ellen wouldn't allow him to sell the house, she would expect to continue living here and be given the same house-keeping money and clothes allowance (what she earned was her own, to be spent as she pleased, sometimes he wondered what she did spend it on). Why should she suffer, she would say with some justice, because he wanted to make a new life for himself?

And, he had to admit, he enjoyed the way Ellen fussed around him. As long as he didn't have to spend too much time with her, he could be flattered by her attentions. Had been from the first time they'd met. He'd been fresh from soon-to-be-abolished National Service, a young salesman with his first foot on the ladder leading to fame and fortune. She was a secretary who had smiled at him shyly when he'd asked for an appointment with her boss, then offered a cup of tea and told him to sit down while she fixed the interview, eyeing him from behind a curtain of curly hair. She had been thrilled at his invitation to go to the cinema. Three years later they had been married.

The headache throbbed relentlessly. Michael gingerly levered himself into an upright position and placed a foot to the floor. He gave himself a moment for the room to settle down around him, then staggered to the bathroom and the Alka Seltzer. He sat on the edge of the bath and waited for clean, pure fizz to make the world better for him.

Where the hell had he been last night? He didn't usually go out Sunday nights, Ellen didn't like it. He closed his eyes and thought carefully. They'd had lunch together, she'd roasted half a leg of lamb, his stomach churned uneasily as he remembered the crisp, fatty skin, then they'd gone for a walk. Ellen had wanted to gather some fir cones to spray gold and silver for Christmas.

That's right! He had carted home a huge basket and reckoned he'd done his bit. He couldn't remember what he'd said but Ellen had lost her temper. Told him now his bit on the side had passed away, he could pay her more attention. At which something had snapped in him. He had a nastily clear vision of Ellen backing away, her mouth working, fright, no, terror in her eyes. What could he have been saying? He only knew he'd wanted to hit her, hit her stupid face, smash in the prissy mouth. It had been all he could do to leave the house without physically assaulting her.

It all came back to him now. He'd gone down to the pub, met up with some of the boys there, and next thing they were on their way to that club at Reading. Damn silly thing to do. How the hell had he got home in one piece? Had they arranged a taxi for him, as Anna had done the other night? Fine mess he'd be in if he lost his licence. How long would Joel Madoc keep a grounded sales director on his board, eh? And if he lost his job, where would all their plans be then?

Moving with extreme care, Michael put the plug in the bath and turned on the taps. Submerged in blissfully warm water, he decided to phone the office and say he wasn't coming in. Let Finer Foods, Anna, and the whole mess go hang. Without Marian none of it seemed worth the effort any more.

The telephone rang. Dripping water by the bedroom extension, Michael told Joel Madoc he was just leaving.

Sooner than he would have thought possible, he was in Joel's office. The man's eyes looked as tired as Michael's felt. The Sales Director decided to take the initiative, strode confidently across the floor, and took the chair on the other side of the partner's desk. It was a mistake.

'I thought we'd sit over here,' said Joel. He rose and led the way to the sitting area. Michael's mood lifted slightly as he saw Darina Lisle there. This must be some sort of discussion on the stupid book, yet another of Joel's mad ideas. Eleanor must have been mentally as well as physically affected by her illness when she brought him into the company.

She had called Michael into her office, this office, late one Friday afternoon. The sun had been streaming in through that window and he had been shocked at how thin and worn she was looking. He'd known she hadn't been well for some time but hadn't realized it could be serious.

She'd told him exactly how ill she was and how important it was for her to know the right person was at the head of the company while she underwent treatment.

He'd thought, of course he'd thought, that she was going to hand over to him. It would have been only right, only just. Hadn't he backed her in every way? Agreed to the principle of the rolling five-year plan, reviewed annually, so they always knew exactly where they were going? Hadn't he scoured the market for new ideas, presenting them to the board with his considered judgement as to whether they would be a success or not? Run the sales force and seen their far-flung chains of stockists were kept supplied and informed of all new lines, were regularly tapped for new ideas? And hadn't it been he who had suggested the sampling sessions with competitors' products?

Of course, he hadn't got it right every time. He'd failed to see what big sellers those Scandinavian crisp rolls were going to be. By the time they'd woken up to that one, crisp rolls were all over the shops. He had also been slow to see the potential in the snack

71

market and he supposed there had been other instances over the years.

But to bring in her husband over his head!

They all knew Joel Madoc, of course. After all, he and Eleanor had been married nearly sixteen years. But the man was involved in his own company, he only blazed briefly through the offices every now and then, spreading charm and bonhomie, when he wanted to see Eleanor for something or other. Or was brought in for a sampling session, you had to admit that the man did have a palate. And once a year Eleanor held a party at their house for all the company and Joel was always the ideal host. More so, by all accounts, than Patrick Cavanagh had been. The tales of his rudeness, not to mention his inability to cope with alcohol, were legendary. But Joel had never struck Michael as more than an elegant clothes peg with a knack for designing menswear. And as for that hideous monstrosity he had insisted on building in the grounds of Harvey Drax's old house, every time the party had been held there Michael had wanted to heave heavy bricks through its plate-glass windows.

'Joel has accepted a marvellous offer for his company and the timing is perfect,' Eleanor explained as his mind whirled with incomprehension, anger, and something else he only later identified as furious jealousy. 'As you must have realized, he knows a lot about Finer Foods.' Michael hadn't realized anything of the sort. 'I have consulted him on so many points over the years, he's familiar with most of what has been going on. I couldn't find anyone I could trust more to manage my company until I'm really better.'

Then she'd turned that limpid smile of hers on him. 'I know I can rely on you, Michael, to back him all the way. I've got such a marvellous team here, he will soon find his feet.'

If she hadn't been so obviously ill, he'd have told her exactly what he thought and given her his resignation. As it was he consoled himself with the thought that it wouldn't be for long.

But Eleanor had not got better. And after her death they found she had left her shares to Joel. That was when Anna had produced her plan.

Michael brought his wandering mind back to the present and realized that Joel was telling him he wanted Darina Lisle to know as much about the company as possible and suggesting he gave her some details of the Chinese restaurant business.

72

'I think it would be a good idea for you to run through a typical day with them, detail what they order, what you discuss. After all, you still call on all the major London restaurants, don't you?' The question was superfluous, the man knew Michael had kept the major accounts under his personal supervision. It was his way of keeping his hand in and knowing something of what was going on at the grass roots. It helped also to flatter the most successful owners. They liked to have the sales director personally taking their order; and the continuity of the same person calling on them year in, year out, satisfied the Chinese love of tradition. But he failed to see how any of this was going to help the tall cookery writer with her book.

'How about taking the last day you spent with them. That would have been Thursday, wouldn't it?'

Light burst through the remains of Michael's headache. For some reason Joel wanted to check his alibi and had chosen this convoluted way of doing it. Well, the Sales Director thought grimly, this should be easy enough. The police had taken him through it in minute detail already.

'Certainly, I'd be delighted,' he said smoothly. 'Just let me get my order book and diary.' He didn't miss the glance exchanged by Joel and Darina as he left the room.

He walked swiftly to his office, his thoughts racing. They couldn't suspect him of electrocuting Marian, could they? But why else this pantomime?

He'd thought his feelings for the Financial Director were common knowledge among the Drax family, that he'd become something of a laughing stock because of them. Could it have something to do with that tag, 'But each man kills the thing he loves'? What a ridiculous sentiment. As if he'd ever want to hurt a hair of Marian's head.

He could remember the first time he'd met her as vividly as if it had been yesterday. He'd been in his third week as salesman with Finer Foods, thrilled to be involved with a firm whose products he really valued, loving getting to grips with the various lines, still unable to believe he was working in a field he enjoyed so much. He'd been taken into the accounts department to meet Harvey Drax's brother, Financial Director in those days. And there she had been, a slight figure with fair hair in a page-boy bob gently framing a face that could have belonged to a medieval princess. Poor Ellen, stoutly pregnant with their second son, never stood a chance after that.

Michael found his diary and order book and returned to Joel's office.

Deliberately, slowly, in full detail, he took them through his Thursday, from one end of Soho to the other, enjoying giving chapter and verse on people seen, orders taken, subjects discussed, even the menu of the late lunch he had had with his old chum who ran one of Soho's most respected Chinese restaurants.

'I checked everyone's supply of soy sauce,' he finished. 'There was one consignment that wasn't right and I've arranged for it to be exchanged.'

'How are we getting on with finding out what went wrong with the sauce?' Joel Madoc appeared slightly punch drunk with the detail that had been thrown his way. He leant back on the sofa, bored and disconsolate; as well he might, thought Michael, more than a little smugly.

'I had a word with Patrick Browne on the phone in Hong Kong. He was going to look into the matter and discuss it with you on Thursday, but I suppose he didn't have a chance?'

'No,' acknowledged Joel. 'I should have rung him at his hotel, but what with the police enquiries and everything, I didn't get round to it. Is he still over here?'

'Afraid not. He rang me at home on Saturday, apologized for not being able to get through to you and said he was off to Europe. I'm afraid my mind was on Marian's death and I forgot to ask him about the sauce.'

'I really need to get together with him. Hong Kong is such an important part of our business, I should know our agent out there. I was only in the warehouse when he arrived, Maggie soon found me. But by that time Marian's body had been discovered and it was too late.'

Too late, it was as if Michael's heart was an anvil and the words were hammers, ringing their message with blows that resounded round his battered brain. If his chances with Marian had been slim before, now they were non-existent.

He gathered up his diary and order book and left the Managing Director's office. He knew Joel wouldn't stop him, he'd got what he wanted and much good would it do him.

Chapter Eleven

'No way he could have made all that up,' said Joel Madoc dispiritedly as the door shut behind Michael Berkeley.

'Or that he could have persuaded all those people to back his story. I was impressed, too, with the way he seems to handle the orders. The restaurants may give him cash but it all appears to be thoroughly documented.'

'That book will be the official one,' Joel said. 'He could easily have another which he uses to invoice to them, with marked up prices, then all he would have to do is pocket the difference. There could be other little arrangements as well, splitting the proceeds of a shortfall in deliveries with some of the staff, for instance. It's not going to be easy to check, he's had their loyalty for many years. It's just another instance of how much we need computerization.' He stretched his arms wearily.

Darina felt he could be placing too much trust in computers. A criminal with ingenuity could circumvent computer safeguards, not to mention finding ways of using its arm's length procedures to advantage.

'I think you have to give up your idea of Michael Berkeley murdering your sister-in-law. An alibi that detailed must stand up, unless the man is a complete idiot.'

'No, Michael's not that. He's a good sales director. A little limited, can't really see far enough ahead to make him top-man material, but first class in every other way. Old Harvey made a good choice there.'

'Did you know your father-in-law well?' Darina thought again of the portrait in the board room, the gimlet eyes and closed mouth.

'Yes, he didn't die until three or four years after we were married.'

'Did you get on well with him?'

'Harvey? Well enough. It might have been different if I'd been involved in the company at that stage but I was, thank Heavens, running my own show. And successfully. After Eleanor's first husband that was such a relief to him I think he was prepared to overlook my various shortcomings.'

'Such as?' Darina wondered if an astute and careful man such as Harvey Drax appeared to have been would have distrusted that Latin charm.

'Well, there was the difference in years for a start. I think he felt Eleanor would live to regret marrying a man ten years younger than herself. And he always suspected any man interested in one of the Drax women of being after their money.'

'The company was successful even then?'

'It was small compared to the business it does today but, yes, it was counted a very successful company. Certainly kept the family in fine style.'

'Is it still a family company?'

'The Draxes and myself own the major part but Eleanor instituted a non-voting employee shareholder scheme. It helps cultivate loyalty and a genuine interest in the company. Everyone who's worked here for more than two years has at least a few shares.'

'And someone like Michael? He's been here a long time, hasn't he?'

'God, yes, approaching twenty years. He has a block of voting shares as well as a sizeable holding of the non-employees' stock.' Joel slanted a glance at Darina from eyes that had assumed his hooded look. 'A lot of questions, can it be that you are becoming interested in investigating Marian's death after all?' He rose and arched his back, easing tired muscles. 'I hope you are, because I've run out of ideas.' He moved over to his desk, sat down, and picked up some papers.

Darina still had a question or two. 'Do you know who Marian will have left her shares to?'

Joel dropped the paper he had been studying. 'The old question, who benefits, eh? As far as I know, if she hasn't changed her will recently, it's Anna.'

'Your step-daughter?'

'My step-daughter,' he repeated without inflection. 'Marian was very fond of her. But in case that gives you ideas, Anna has just

76

as cast-iron an alibi as Michael. She was also in London, with our advertising agents discussing a new campaign. She rang the marketing department about some point or other and they had to ring back with information, gave it to her personally. There's no doubt that she was there.'

'She must find food a bit different from the fashion industry,' fished Darina. Then, as Joel didn't seem to respond, she added, 'I understand she started her career as a buyer in one of the large stores.'

'That's right,' said Joel heavily. 'She was a good one, too. I don't think her heart is involved with Finer Foods the way it was with fashion.'

'She seems committed enough,' commented Darina.

'Oh, she enjoys the business side but she's not actually interested in the products themselves. I was surprised to find she was entering the recipe competition, I dread to think what the dish is like.'

'She isn't interested in food?' Darina was shocked. Food to her was more than fuel to keep the body going, it was a delight and never-ending fascination. After all, if something was so vitally important to one's very existence, it made sense not only to know as much as possible about it but also to enjoy the infinite variety of ways it could be produced and presented. For someone to be closely involved in the food world and not to have that interest and commitment was hard for her to understand.

The door of Joel's office opened and Detective Chief Inspector Melville stood there. 'I wonder if we could ask you a few more questions, sir?'

Darina disappeared and took herself off home. Finer Foods' offices were clogged with investigating policemen and there was little to be gained from trying to research products under those conditions. She spent the rest of the week working on recipes at home and looking forward to her visit to Jane's delicatessen on Friday.

But on the Thursday Jane rang and said they'd have to postpone it for a week, she was going to be too busy after all. 'Why not bring your fiancé over for a meal at the weekend?' she suggested instead. 'Joel swears he won't talk shop or mention the investigation.'

Darina smiled to herself. For Joel not to mention either Marian's murder or Finer Foods, his mouth would have to be stitched together. He would stoop to any deception to get William involved.

'I'm sorry but we can't,' she said. 'We're off to Gloucestershire, to spend the weekend with my future parents-in-law.' She put down the telephone and sat looking at it for a moment. She never would have thought she could be grateful to be able to say that.

Chapter Twelve

It was a glorious morning, crisp and clear with autumnal leaves glowing in the October sunshine.

Darina stood by a five-bar gate leading via a path into a wood. The air was so still, so silent, she could have been alone in the world. In fact, though, the scene was thronged with riders and spectators.

As immobile on their horses as statues, members of the Pigrams' local hunt were arranged in a circle round the wood. Standing back from them were the hunt followers, some leaning on sticks, some shuffling their feet in fallen leaves, some standing in suitable spots on the grass verges of fields planted with winter wheat.

'It's cubbing tomorrow morning,' Lieutenant Colonel Pigram had said. 'We'll be covering our wood. If the weather's as half-way decent as we hope, it should be fun for you to come along.'

Deep in the wood the watchers heard the baying of hounds. 'They've found,' said William. Darina moved closer to him. She felt marvellous. The air was like the champagne they'd drunk the previous night. She drew a deep breath and felt it fill her lungs. How could she have been dreading this weekend? It was wonderful to be away from all William's new responsibilities and the mysteries surrounding Finer Foods.

They hardly seemed to have seen each other recently; if they weren't careful they would grow into strangers.

For a time it had seemed that becoming engaged meant little more than a formalization of their previous relationship. They were already living together, what difference did a ring on the finger make?

A lot, Darina was finding out. It wasn't just that she had made a commitment, stated to herself and the world that this was the man she wanted to share the rest of her life with, she had let the world into their lives. Anyone now seemed to have the right to ask questions and give advice. Becoming engaged, it appeared, was not just one decision, it was a prelude to a thousand and one other decisions. Questions were flung at them from all sides. When were they going to be married, what sort of wedding was it going to be, who should be invited, where were they going to spend the honeymoon, where were they going to live? These were not considered decisions solely for her and William to make, these were matters their families and friends felt they had every right to share.

For the first time in her life, Darina was grateful her family only consisted of her mother. William came more highly equipped. Both parents living, a beloved uncle and aunt, two brothers and two sisters. His status as eldest son had not inhibited his siblings from descending the moment the engagement was announced and handing out diktats with exuberant enthusiasm.

Sarah, William's younger sister, wanted to be bridesmaid, of course. Darina had no quarrel with that, she liked her future sister-in-law, and her tall, dark good looks would complement her own fairness and even greater height nicely. The boys, as William called them, had ribald advice on how to control 'the Amazon', as Darina was dubbed (a marginal improvement, she felt, on 'Valkyrie', which was what Robert, the elder of the two, had called her on their first meeting; but Richard, the younger, had insisted she lacked proper Wagnerian stridency, a remark that immediately endeared him to Darina and enabled her to bear the alternative nickname with fortitude). She had yet to meet William's other sister, older than himself and married to an Army officer.

Last night had inevitably led to a run through of such wedding arrangements as had been proposed, together with the kindest of suggestions that they get a move on.

'Not set a date yet?' had been the Colonel's tactful way of introducing the subject.

'Sssh, darling, that's something for William and Darina to settle, it's not our business,' came from Joyce Pigram, who rather spoilt the effect by adding, 'I'm sure Mrs Lisle isn't interfering like this, is she, Darina, dear?'

Darina had been prepared to smile gently and let the matter slide. Her fiancé had other ideas. 'Not interfering? You must be joking! She's on the telephone several times a week to see if we've come to a decision. I think she's afraid if Darina doesn't tie me down soon, I'll change my mind!'

Darina had allowed him to squeeze her hand but bent her mind to exacting revenge later that night.

'Well, naturally, she's looking forward to welcoming you into her family just as much as I am to having Darina share our life,' was Joyce Pigram's diplomatic comment.

'So what's holding matters up?' pressed John Pigram. 'You're both of age, presumably there's no just cause or impediment why you shouldn't get on with it, I don't see what the problem is?'

There had been a little silence William made no move to fill. Darina had sat with both John and Joyce Pigram's gaze fastened on her.

She had murmured something about William's new job but they all knew it wasn't that.

'Well, my advice, not that you need it, I'm sure' – Joyce Pigram flashed her scintillating smile – 'is not to hang about too long. Engagements, in my experience, hold dreadful pitfalls.'

'Your experience?' hooted her husband. 'You've been holding out on me, I thought I was your one and only fiancé!'

'Darina knows exactly what I mean.' His wife had been imperturbable. 'You've got to move on in life. Engagements are a bus stop but if you think it doesn't matter how long you wait there, that another will be along every few minutes, you may find that service has been suspended.'

'Oh, Ma, what a way of putting it!'

Her smile to her son had been kindly. 'Laugh, if you will, darling, I know what I'm talking about.'

Joyce Pigram displayed, in fact, an enviable confidence in all her doings.

Her son had once declared his mother was a hopeless cook. Dinner the first night was delicious. When Darina complimented her, she said, without apology, that a delicatessen in her little local town had provided it. 'They sell splendid "meals to go"; all you have to do is follow the reheating instructions. Makes Marks and Spencer look like McDonald's.'

When William, with professional interest, asked after her doings on the magistrates' bench, she related details of current cases with cool competence.

Darina knew that Joyce Pigram was also Chairman of the county Conservative Association and had been a district councillor.

'I believe in doing my bit,' she said to Darina. 'But I never let my family suffer. John has never had to get a meal himself all the time we've been married, or iron his own shirt.' Darina told herself she was imagining the way her eyes had fallen on William, she couldn't possibly tell that his shirts were only nicely folded after a session in the tumble-drier.

The evening had ended with a riotous game of Scrabble, Joyce Pigram winning by a wide margin. It was after that Darina had discovered that the room to which she had been shown on arrival was to be hers alone, that William was to spend the night in his old bedroom down another corridor in the Pigrams' spacious house.

Her room had been comfortable, with its own bathroom. It looked out over beautiful countryside, was equipped with every comfort, including a jar of biscuits, a dish of fruit, the latest magazines, two fluffy bathrobes, and a large double bed. Darina could not believe it was intended for single occupancy.

She had waited for some time for William to join her. He had kissed her lingeringly at the foot of the stairs when she had pleaded tiredness some time after midnight, then had gone back into the drawing room. When she had carefully opened her bedroom door a little later, she had heard male voices rising and falling. She had retreated back to bed and opened the new *Vogue* for an enjoyable read while she waited.

Now in the crisp air she snuggled against William's side and asked: 'Why didn't you come and join me last night? You didn't even open my door to see if I was still awake.'

He put his arm round her shoulders and held her close. 'And how do you know that?'

'My light was still on this morning and the magazine I was reading was on the floor. If you'd looked in on me, you'd have turned off the one and picked up the other.'

'My own little detective,' he said good-humouredly. 'I must never try and hide things from you. I thought you realized I was saying goodnight when you went up.'

'It never occurred to me you wouldn't be joining me later.'

'My fault, I should have explained Ma is really very old-fashioned about things like sharing bedrooms before one is married.'

'But she knows we are living together, and it's not as though we are teenagers. I'm nearly thirty!'

Baying of hounds floated across to them. William smiled. 'Nothing you can say will convince my mother to change her rule

82

that the only unmarried couples to share a bedroom in her house are those of the same sex.'

'How does she test for heterosexuality?' murmured Darina, but low enough for William to be able to ignore.

She sighed and settled down again to watch the non-activity that seemed to consist of cub hunting. The aim, John Pigram had explained, was to train the hounds and, if she had understood aright, the foxes. No doubt lots was going on in the wood but out here it all looked very dull. The main activity was a setter cross sniffing interestedly at someone else's Labrador and deciding he should be seen off the territory. His owner dragged the growling and struggling animal away, towards Darina and William, opening up a strategic distance between the two dogs.

As he got closer, Darina recognized the dog's owner. 'Charles!' she cried.

Her publisher turned. 'Darina,' he exclaimed with delight. 'What on earth are you doing here?'

'I could ask you the same question.'

'I live here,' came the unexpected answer. 'That is to say, I'm a weekender. This, I take it, is your famous detective sergeant fiancé?'

'No,' said Darina proudly, 'my famous detective *inspector* fiancé.' She introduced William. After a few minutes conversation Charles said, 'I think this is as much as I can take of such static entertainment, why don't you two come back for a drink? It's just about a respectable hour. You can meet my daughters.'

'Really, Charles,' said Darina as they followed him along a path towards a group of cars, 'you're one surprise after another. First it's a country hideaway when I'd always marked you down as someone unable to exist outside London, and now daughters! I thought you just had a small son.'

'Jeremy is the fruit of my second marriage, the twins belong to my first. I get them every other *exeat*. Collected them early this morning, I thought they'd be interested in the cub hunt but the call of the video was too strong. I should have insisted, I suppose, but I was so delighted that this terrible business with their aunt doesn't seem to have made too strong an impression that I left them to it and brought this dreadful animal out for his exercise.' The dreadful animal was trotting nicely beside his master. As they reached the cars, he stood quietly waiting for Charles to open the door of his, then leaped neatly on to the back seat.

'What terrible business?' asked Darina.

He turned in surprise. 'Why, Marian Drax's murder, of course? You must know all about it.'

'But what is your connection?' Darina clutched William's hand and realized exactly what it was just before Charles's answer came, a trifle stiffly she thought.

'I thought you understood, Anna Drax is my ex-wife. Marian was my aunt-in-law.'

As William drove off after Charles's car, Darina complained, 'He might have told me! How was I to guess that the Johnson bit of Anna's name meant Charles?'

'It's too bad,' agreed her fiancé. 'The moment he heard of Marian Drax's death, he should have rung and made sure you realized so you could interrogate him on everything he knew about his ex-aunt-in-law.'

'Sometimes, William,' Darina said with awful calm, 'you can be such a brute.'

Their journey ended in front of a charming stone house in the Cotswold style, standing sturdily under its gabled roof in a neat garden. As they entered, a slight woman with thick dark hair, wearing trousers and a puffa jacket, emerged from the back of the house. Charles introduced his wife; Rosemary gave Darina and William a delightful smile then turned to her husband.

'I'm so glad you're back, darling, I must pop down to the village and get one or two things, I'll join you later.' She took the car keys off Charles and disappeared out of the front door.

Charles led the way into a living room serviceably furnished with little attempt at style. Draped over a floral linen-covered sofa were two girls some eight or nine years old. Dressed in jeans and sweat-shirts advertising some pop group, long fair hair streaming in all directions, they were screaming with delight at what was playing on the television screen.

Charles turned off the set to squawks of protest. 'Hey, Dad, we're watching that!'

'Hush, kids, we have visitors. Darina, William, let me introduce Kate and Isabel.'

Long legs slid down the sofa back as the two girls righted themselves. Laughter and protest both died out of their eyes, they got up politely and extended identical hands to the visitors.

They looked very like their mother, their facial bone structure was exactly the same, and in their quickly assumed formality Darina thought she could see Anna's cool composure.

'Miss Lisle is writing a book on Finer Foods' products,' said their father after he had got them to fetch ice and lemon and had supplied everyone with drinks, the twins clutching cans of Coke and sitting either side of their father on the sofa, a head against each of his shoulders.

The news appeared unspectacular until Kate, or it could have been Isabel, straightened with sudden interest. 'Darina Lisle? Wasn't it you who found Aunt Marian?'

'Well, I was there, yes.'

'Gosh!' Two matching pairs of eyes regarded her with awe.

'Do,' pleaded Isabel, or it could have been Kate, 'tell us *everything*. Everybody else clams up and won't tell us a thing.'

'Kids, Miss Lisle does not want to be quizzed about a very nasty experience. And I can't believe you can be so heartless and gruesome. I thought you were fond of Aunt Marian!'

The girls looked shamefaced. 'Sorry, Dad. It's just, just . . .'

'Just that everyone treats us as such babies! Mummy says we can't go to the funeral and won't answer any questions. And all you will tell us is that Aunt Marian is in heaven!' The scorn with which that was uttered said volumes for the religious instruction at their no doubt expensive school. 'We get taught all about sex now, I don't see why we can't hear about people dying.'

A stunned silence greeted this and Darina wondered if they weren't older than she had originally thought.

'Your aunt was electrocuted, in the Finer Foods' kitchen,' said Darina at last as Charles seemed unable to come to grips with the situation.

A little silence as the two girls absorbed that, then, 'What does that mean? Something to do with electricity?'

'Yes. You know if you are foolish enough to stick your hand in a light bulb socket you get a shock?'

The two heads nodded.

'Well, that's more or less what happened to your aunt, except she got a very much greater charge of electricity. In some way we don't understand, the metal sinks in the kitchen were wired up so that if you touched both at the same time you got a very bad shock. Unfortunately your aunt did touch them and she died.'

The twins considered this information.

'Would we get a shock if we did the washing up?' asked one.

'No,' Darina assured her quickly. 'Your sinks are quite different.'

'But if we did the washing up at the office?' asked the other.

'Still be all right, it's all been made safe now.'

'But how did it be made unsafe?'

'That is what the police are trying to find out.'

'William is a policeman,' said their father. The eyes swivelled their gaze in a new direction.

'Are you a detective?'

He nodded.

'And will you find out how the sinks were elec, elec, electrocuted?'

William explained he wasn't involved, that he worked in a different police force and told them a little about a burglary case he was working on. But it didn't prove much of a diversion.

'First Madre died,' said Kate, Darina was almost sure she had the twins correctly identified. 'And then Aunt Marian. I don't like people dying.'

Their father hugged them more closely. 'We all die eventually, poppet.'

'But you're not going to for ages and ages, are you?'

'Not for ages and ages, nor is your mother.'

'I suppose Padre Joel might die soon, he's pretty old,' said Kate.

Darina was glad Joel wasn't there.

'Well, Aunt Marian won't be marrying him now, anyway,' Isabel announced.

'What did you say?' exclaimed Charles. 'Who told you she was going to?'

'You know it was a secret, silly!' That was Kate, leaning across her father to give her twin a none-too-gentle dig in the ribs.

Her sister aimed a punch back, ably deflected by her father. 'Whoa, stop this or you go upstairs. Now, tell me exactly what put this idea into your heads.'

He looked sternly at his daughters, holding each a little away from him by a shoulder apiece. After a moment Isabel said a little sulkily, 'It was Maria. In the Easter holidays, after Madre died. She had her friend round, fat Pat with the spots, and they were talking. And fat Pat said, "What is the divine Joel going to do now, then?" And Maria said that Marian had her claws well and truly into him, just as if she was a cat. And so when fat Pat had gone I asked Maria what she meant by Aunt Marian having claws and she said' – Isabel gazed at her father, wide eyed and innocent – 'she said it was just a joke, just a way of saying someone was

86

going to marry someone but it was a secret and I mustn't mention it to anyone.'

'I said I didn't believe it,' asserted Kate.

'And why didn't you?' asked her father.

'Because you only get married when you're young. Padre Joel is much too old.'

'Silly, lots of people get married when they're old,' said her sister.

'Of course they don't,' repeated Kate.

'William and I are going to get married,' put in Darina.

Kate looked at them both, her head on one side, shining fair hair hanging in a waterfall. 'Well,' she said kindly, 'I don't think you're *very* old. Probably not too old to get married, anyway. Can we be bridesmaids?'

Chapter Thirteen

Charles promptly sent both girls upstairs, but not before Darina had promised them they should be bridesmaids. The thought of the two pretty girls following her up the aisle was irresistible. Kate stopped at the living-room door and looked back at her, 'We'll come down later, before you go,' she promised. 'So you can tell us about the wedding.'

'Go, you shameless hussy!' shouted Charles.

Upstairs a baby started to cry. 'Now look what you've done,' said Kate. 'That's Jeremy. And we had such trouble to get him off, Isabel and me. Well, I suppose I had better go and see what I can do.' She tossed her hair back over her shoulder with great authority and left the room.

'Are they fond of their little brother?' asked Darina.

'Adore him. Rosemary very sensibly involved them as soon as she knew she was pregnant. She's been just great with the girls. She wanted to tell them all about Marian, said they needed to know but I thought they were too young. I shall have to tell her I was wrong.' He sighed. 'Remember what they say, if ever you distrust your wife's judgement, just remember who she married! Now, tell me about your wedding plans. And don't worry about the twins, I'll get Rosemary to explain to Kate they can't go hiring themselves out as bridesmaids.'

Darina said she really did want to have them but as yet they hadn't set a date.

Rosemary returned just as Darina and William were refusing a third drink and saying they should be going.

Her face fell. 'Oh, don't leave before I've had a chance to meet you properly. Do you have any plans for lunch, or can you join us? It's only nursery food but there's plenty of it.'

At the same time as Darina tried to explain they were staying with William's parents, he said they'd love to stay. 'Ma and Dad won't be back for ages yet.'

'That's settled, then.' Charles reached for their glasses. William said he'd switch to beer and Darina followed Rosemary into the kitchen, offering to lay the table.

Didn't she find it difficult running two homes, she asked her hostess, setting out stainless-steel cutlery on the nice old pine kitchen table.

'Calls for a certain amount of organization but it's so good to get out of London at the weekend. Especially when we have the girls. This is much closer to collect them from school and it's easier to keep them out of mischief. Kate's into everything and Isabel follows her lead.'

Rosemary gave Darina a warm smile. 'I really am so pleased to meet you, I always read your cookery column.' She placed a fish pie in the microwave, put a saucepan of water on to boil, and found a packet of frozen peas. 'I'm sure you're far too nice to ask personal questions but Charles has told me how you solved those other murders and if I were in your shoes I'd be dying to know about him and Anna.'

Darina sat down on one of the kitchen chairs and laughed. 'I'll give you a reference for the mind-reading business any day.'

'Charles hates talking about it but, as he's always telling me, I have bags of sense but no sensibility.' She took the peas over to the stove and stood waiting for the water to boil. 'Perhaps it would be best to start with where I came in. I was his secretary. I never meant to fall in love with Charles, reckoned I was much too sensible for that. It sort of crept up on me. He was always coming into the office with buttons off his shirt, suit needing cleaning, all that sort of thing. I got used to organizing his appearance as well as his desk. Then the twins were born and he was crazy about them, he was just so sweet! But gradually I started to realize that all wasn't well at home. By the time the girls had their first birthday, he was coming into the office all tensed up, snapping at everyone, quite unlike what he'd been when I first started with the company. By the end of the day I'd have got him calmed down, almost relaxed, only to find next morning he was just as bad. It was when I realized that any sane person would hand in their notice rather than have to put up with some of the treatment he was meting out that I recognized what I should have been aware of much earlier.'

'That you'd fallen in love with him?'

'Too right. Then I forgot something stupid one evening, came back to the office, and found him crying. It was too much, this lovely man sitting at his desk with tears streaming down his face, unable to face going home. I just took him in my arms and said there, there, everything would be all right. And somehow it was!' There was a reminiscent smile on her face. 'Gradually I got the story out of him. Anna is the original ice queen. He'd married her thinking she was sleeping beauty and he was the prince who was going to kiss her awake. As the years wore on, he'd begun to despair of ever really getting through to her but reckoned they were reasonably happy. She had an interesting job, so did he, they had a good social life and everything rubbed along. Then Anna got pregnant and gave up her job but being a housewife and mother just sent her round the bend. She has absolutely no talent for either.'

'Why didn't she hire someone to look after that side and go back to work herself?'

'I don't really know, but I think she felt it would be admitting failure of some sort. She struggled along getting more and more depressed and in more and more of a mess. Charles was just desperate and terribly worried about the girls. He couldn't see how things were going to get any better. He said it was only coming into the office that kept him sane and he could understand how Anna could get in such a state without one to go to herself.'

Darina could also see how the sight of Rosemary's calm and cheerful face, her warmth and understanding, could have made the office far more than a peaceful retreat.

'So when he found that he'd fallen in love with you, he made the break?'

Rosemary gave a wry smile. 'It wasn't quite that easy. He felt the most monumental guilt. He dithered between the two of us for nearly a year. Finally I said I couldn't take any more and that I was going to leave. He didn't say anything and I handed in my resignation. I had to give a month's notice and that month was the worst of my life. Charles was absolutely foul, I was in tears half the time and by the last day I couldn't face coming in and just rang and said I was ill and could they post my P45 and my money from the pension fund. I'd been feeling so dreadful I hadn't made any attempt to get another job and I sat in my flat in an awful dressing gown, trying to stop crying and wondering what I was going to do with my life. And suddenly there was Charles at the door, saying he couldn't live without me and could we please get married! Talk about the world turning technicolour!' Rosemary gave a little laugh and added frozen peas to boiling water.

'Had you met Anna at all?'

'Only when she came into the office. It always depressed me because she looked so lovely. She has the most amazing sense of style. We had more contact when it came to making arrangements over the twins. I can't say she was friendly but she managed to be civilized.

'It was Eleanor who made me understand Anna, at least, partly, I don't think anyone could understand her totally.'

'Eleanor Drax?'

'Right. After the wedding she asked me to lunch. She was an amazing woman. She told me straight out that she didn't approve of Charles's behaviour but could understand that he'd come to the end of his tether and that, since I'd be having such a lot to do with the children, she thought it was best to tell me something about their mother. Then she said it was her fault that Anna found personal relationships so difficult.'

Rosemary drained the peas, placed them in a dish, and added a knob of butter. The microwave pinged the end of its programme. She looked at her watch, then at Darina, placed all the food in the oven and came and sat down at the kitchen table with her guest.

'Eleanor told me she would never be able to stop blaming herself for ruining Anna's life.'

'How?'

'She'd stolen Joel Madoc from her.'

'Joel?'

'Apparently Anna brought him home to meet her mother. Eleanor says she hadn't been told he was somebody special but that she should have known, Anna hardly ever brought anyone home. But when they arrived, Anna couldn't have appeared less interested, seemed to be regretting the fact she'd asked him. It seems they'd met at a promotion in the store where she was working. Did you know he had his own shirt business?'

'I knew it was some sort of men's fashion.'

'He designed really great shirts. Charles has several, marvellous styling, beautifully made, very expensive. So there was this desperately attractive man, said Eleanor, looking lost and a bit forlorn, abandoned by Anna. She did her best to entertain him, her best turned out to be sensationally good, and everything went on from there. Eleanor must have been all of ten years older than Joel but, until towards the end, she looked so marvellous you didn't really notice the age gap.

'It wasn't until several years after Anna had married Charles,' Eleanor said, 'that she found out she had broken her heart over the way Joel had dropped her after that first visit and that she'd finally married hoping she'd grow into love. Eleanor told me she would never forgive herself for the way she had ignored any possibility that Anna might have had prior claim. She just fell under Joel's spell and that was that.'

'How awful!' Darina thought of Anna's cool exterior, her impeccable style, and of the antagonism she now displayed towards her step-father. How she must have buried her feelings. No wonder Charles hadn't been able to kiss the sleeping beauty awake.

'Just what I thought.' Rosemary paused and looked straight at Darina. 'I've told you all this because there's something else I want to tell you. Something nobody else knows, not even Charles. I don't know if it has any significance, but ever since I've heard about poor Marian's death, it's been worrying me.' She fiddled with the knives and forks on the table and Darina waited, trying to look encouraging.

'It was while Eleanor was so ill. Joel was invited to make a speech to some conference or other, I can't remember what exactly but apparently it was very important, the sort of thing you don't turn down. He asked Anna to go with him and she rang and asked could they possibly stay the night. Charles was in the States on business and I didn't see any reason why not, when the twins aren't with us we've got two spare rooms and Joel has often stayed when he's been in town late.

'They arrived with Anna looking radiant. Joel was drawn and pale, not surprising with trying to run the company and having to watch Eleanor fail to respond to treatment. They went off to the dinner with Anna behaving just like a girl on her first date. I was in bed before they got back but in the morning Joel went off on business and Anna had breakfast with me. She couldn't wait to give every detail of the evening, how well Joel's speech had gone down, how marvellous he'd been, what a wonderful time they'd had. I could hardly believe this was Anna. All her coolness was gone, evaporated, she was lively, fun. I thought if she'd given Charles half a glimpse of the girl she could be, no wonder he'd made such an effort with her. Then, all at once, she stopped talking, looked me straight in the eye, and said she didn't begrudge Charles and me our happiness any more.'

'Meaning she thought she'd found some of her own?' asked

Darina as Rosemary seemed to have come to a full stop and was sitting staring at the wall.

'What?' Charles's second wife pulled herself out of her reverie. 'I'm sorry, I was just remembering how she looked when she said that, just like Kate or Isabel when they're playing with Jeremy sometimes. Well, I couldn't help asking Anna how Eleanor was, as though I didn't know, because it seemed so awful to me that her daughter thought true happiness was going to come through her death.'

'What happened?'

'She burst into tears. And it all came out. How she'd blamed her mother all these years for robbing her of her chance of real happiness. And how now she really didn't want her to die and felt so guilty in one way but madly happy in another because it looked as though Joel was going to turn to her again.'

'But you can't marry your stepfather, can you?' asked Darina. 'I know they've been talking about changing the law, but has it happened yet?'

'Anna couldn't care less about anything like that,' said Rosemary.

'But you know Joel's just got engaged?'

Rosemary stared at her. 'No!'

'To a nice woman called Jane Leslie. About the same age as Anna, I'd say.'

'Oh, poor girl.' Rosemary thought for a moment. 'When did this happen, before Marian's death?'

'Yes, about a couple of weeks before. Why, is that important?'

'In a way. It means what I was going to tell you is no longer important.'

'Tell me anyway.'

'Well, it was just that next time I collected the girls, Anna had completely reverted to her old difficult self. I tried as tactfully as I could to ask what had happened and finally she turned on me, told me to stop bleating at her and forget she'd ever said anything.'

'No explanation?'

'None. But Isabel told me something that made me wonder.'

'Ah, about fat Pat and Aunt Marian getting her claws into Padre Joel?'

'You know about that?'

'It came out this morning. But do you seriously think Anna could have murdered Marian?'

'It sounds horrible when you say it like that. But you've never seen Anna the way Charles has. And I know from the girls that she has the most incredible temper. Sometimes they're really scared of her. In the early days, Charles was terrified she was going to do one of them some damage, eventually he managed to insist she got a trained nanny to look after them and he talked with Eleanor about encouraging her to get some sort of job. Once she was working again, things got much better.'

'Is Maria the trained nanny?'

'Heavens, no. That all finished when the girls went to boarding school. Since then it's been a succession of au pairs. Maria's the current one, quite a little minx.'

'Do you think she was making it up, about Marian and Joel?'

'What would have been the point? No, as far as men are concerned she's got antennae that would beat Telstar. I wouldn't be surprised if she hadn't made a play for Joel herself. I caught her making eyes at Charles one weekend she was here with the girls. And Joel is no saint where women are concerned. Eleanor seemed to understand she had to turn a blind eye every now and then. He was devoted to her but apparently needed what you might call a little bit extra every now and then.'

The kitchen door opened and Kate stood there. 'Rosie, Dad says to ask you if we are ever going to get any lunch?'

Isabel appeared behind her twin, staggering slightly under the load of a beaming baby. 'Jeremy wants his lunch, Rosie. He was crying and wouldn't go to sleep again so I got him up.' The baby gurgled and held out his arms to his mother.

Rosemary went and took him. 'Thanks, dear, I should have fed him ages ago, I've been chatting with Darina. Do you think I should give him his meal before we have ours?' She looked at the girls.

'Dad will have a fit if he has to wait any longer,' warned Kate. She pulled out a high chair. 'Let's all eat now and I'll feed him.' She went to a cupboard and looked at an assembly of baby foods. 'I'll give him a chicken dinner, he likes that.'

Darina watched her take charge and wondered whether it was her mother or her grandmother that she took after. It certainly wasn't her father!

Chapter Fourteen

William and Darina were in the dog house. Joyce Pigram had got home after the cub hunt to find the lunch she had so carefully arranged for them was still sitting on the dining-room table.

'Of course it doesn't matter,' she said, clearing it away with noisy efficiency after they had returned. 'It was only cold meat after all. But I had prepared a salad and if I'd known you weren't going to be in . . . but, there, as I said, it doesn't matter.' She turned a bright smile on them as she wrapped clingfilm over the bowl of salad. 'Now, tell me all about your lunch, what fun you met a friend.'

Then, when she heard it was Darina's publisher, 'Well, we shall have to have them over for your next weekend with us, funny we haven't met them before. We know practically everyone around here.'

'They only come down for weekends,' Darina said. 'Charles has a flat in Richmond.'

'Oh, weekenders! Still, I don't understand why we haven't run into them. Presumably they must do *some* socializing?'

Darina thought about the happy little household, the books overflowing everywhere, Rosemary's haphazard housekeeping, her interest in Charles's work, the twins' doings, the baby, the garden. 'I'm not sure they do,' she said. 'I think weekends are a rest for them, Charles is always having to see people in London.'

The thought that anyone might want to come down and not meet people, the 'right people' of course, was such an alien one, Joyce Pigram was unable to contemplate it for more than a moment. She gave Darina a brief stare, then pushed the inconvenient Johnsons out of her mind. Several of the Pigrams' close friends had been asked to dinner that evening to meet the happy couple. 'And since I know what an excellent cook you are, dear, I wonder if you wouldn't mind helping me out a tiny bit in the kitchen? Just with one or two little things?'

Darina was delighted there was an opportunity to recover some lost ground. Then found 'one or two little things' turned into preparing most of the meal. It was a hazard of being a cook. Apart from her old friends and a few genuinely understanding folk, those hostesses who were brave enough to ask her to dine tended to react in one of three ways: by attempting to outdo her; ducking the issue altogether by going out to eat or hiring a caterer; or offloading some of the responsibility for the meal on to her, even if it was only advice on whether the meat was done.

Still, it proved to be an enjoyable evening with interesting people, lots to eat and drink, and a happy atmosphere. Darina saw Joyce Pigram at her best, relaxing with good friends, witty, forceful in a way that brought out the best in her guests, an excellent hostess, allowing her husband and son to tease her, and showing off William's fiancée with every appearance of real delight. Once again Darina warmed towards her. And once again she spent a lonely night in her comfortable bedroom.

After a ten o'clock morning service, William and Darina took the dogs for a walk across the common. William's father started out with them but peeled off to visit someone to arrange the local Conservative Association's annual meeting. Joyce Pigram had stayed behind to cook lunch. She had refused Darina's offer of help. 'I wouldn't dream of it, my dear, you did enough last night. Roasting a leg of lamb is just within my capabilities, so you go off and have a nice walk, blow the cobwebs away.'

It was another bright morning, crisp and clear. William released the two Labradors from their leads and threw a couple of sticks. He smiled at Darina. 'Enjoying yourself?'

'Of course!' She tucked her arm into his, hugging it against her, then said, 'I hope I'm going to be a satisfactory daughter-in-law.'

'Is there any doubt?'

After a moment Darina said slowly, 'I think your mother would find it difficult to accept that anyone was good enough for her eldest son, and I can't say I blame her.'

'Ah!'

William found another stick to throw for the dogs. Watching them run after and search for it he said, 'Ma wasn't allowed to go to university or become qualified for a proper career. Dad says she wanted to be a lawyer. She swears she has had the best possible life but part of her has been wasted and she knows it.'

'What stopped her?'

'Her father didn't believe in careers for girls.'

'What age are we talking about? Pre-First World War?'

'It wasn't as easy as you might think. Even in the fifties, she said, girls like her didn't go against their parents. She made the best of things, started doing voluntary work, then met my father and made being an Army wife a career in itself.

'She's managed to convince herself so thoroughly that her life has been completely fulfilling, she finds it extremely difficult to admit there's another way of being a wife and mother. My sisters battle with her all the time.'

Sarah had just qualified as a solicitor, was going to work at the European Commission, she had specialized in European law. The elder, Heather, was stationed with her Army husband in Hong Kong but had just managed to complete a long-range doctorate in history.

'I think she was hoping I'd find someone to marry who had the same idea of family life she has,' William continued. 'Instead, she finds you are just like her daughters.'

At least, Darina thought, I now know where that strong streak of male chauvinism you are managing to conquer so nicely comes from. And what I shall have to cope with in the future from my mother-in-law.

William bent and took the stick a panting dog was offering and threw it again, the light wood spinning in the still air.

All at once Darina knew, without a shadow of a doubt, that she wanted to get married quite soon. It was, as Joyce Pigram had said, time for their relationship to move on.

Before she could say anything, William reverted to an earlier comment. 'Of course, we've hardly got away from things altogether.'

'Meaning?'

'Meaning the Drax murder seems to have followed us.'

Darina took a moment to realize he was referring to Kate's bit of gossip about Marian and Joel.

'Ah, that!' she said, then remembered she hadn't told him any of the details about Anna and Joel she had heard from Rosemary.

'Your Joel Madoc sounds quite a Lothario,' he commented after she'd finished. 'Have you any idea how genuine his feelings for this Jane Leslie are?'

'He appears very much in love with her and she seems dotty about him.'

'Do you think he could have had something going with Marian Drax?'

'How can I tell? But you should have heard the way he spoke to her at that lunch, pressing her on the computerization of the accounts. It was all most embarrassing.'

'How did she react?'

'Wounded, full of justification, angry. Yes, there could have been something personal in it. It may just be the benefit of hindsight, but I'd say she sounded bitter and not just because her job efficiency was being questioned. But when Anna attacked him, she drew back, wouldn't side with her.'

'And you said she made some sort of threat when she heard about the engagement?'

'It was terribly vague but there was that one moment when both Joel and Jane seemed to take it seriously. Then, as I told you, Joel turned it into a joke and that seemed to be that.'

Darina was dismissive, she wanted to discuss more important matters than the mystery of Marian Drax's death. She turned to William. 'How about us getting down to setting a date?'

Lunch was devoted to wedding plans. Darina refused to consider getting married before she had finished the Finer Foods book.

'Yes, dear, you want to get all that out of the way, don't you? After all, you won't want to work after marriage.'

Darina looked at her future mother-in-law in disbelief.

'Ma, Darina will continue with her career,' William said quietly but with an odd little note in his voice. 'After all, with my crazy hours, she'd find herself twiddling her thumbs half the time if she didn't have her own work.'

'Well, I suppose it's sensible enough until babies come along,' conceded his mother.

Confrontation or a gradual campaign of education, which was it to be? Darina was considering her options when Colonel Pigram added his contribution. 'My dear, what would you have felt if you hadn't been allowed to work for the Conservatives, sit on the bench, or do all the other splendid works you are so brilliant at?'

Joyce Pigram gave a little snort. 'Quite different, darling, all that's voluntary and the family has always come first.'

'I'm sure Darina isn't suggesting anything else.' He looked across at the tall girl with eyes so like his son's she couldn't help but smile back at him.

'William and I are a partnership,' she said. 'We believe in helping each other as much as we can. There are no demarcation lines, we work together at running the home.'

'I'm a dab hand at ironing shirts and perfectly capable of producing a meal, even though I live with a fabulous cook. It's nice for her to get an evening off every now and then without having to pay for an expensive restaurant meal. And I certainly don't mind pushing the vacuum cleaner and duster around. I really don't see why I should get all the fun of an interesting career and my wife should be cooped up just doing housework and looking after children.'

Darina pressed his foot under the table with hers and sent him a silent message of thanks. It was the first time she had heard him support her so thoroughly.

Joyce Pigram opened her mouth, closed it again and flushed brick red. She looked across at Darina, meeting her gaze with an effort. 'I'm sorry, I shouldn't have asked you to do all that cooking last night, I never thought.'

She looked so uncomfortable, Darina forgave her immediately. 'It was fun, honestly. You gave us such a nice evening and it made me feel part of the family.' She wondered briefly why she hadn't felt that at the time. For a moment there was real communication between her and Joyce Pigram.

Then her hostess said, 'What I can't understand is why you are bothering with this booklet, book, whatever it is. I thought you were a proper cook, into preparing fresh foods, worrying about nutrition, and all those things we are told are so important these days. Not descending like the rest of us to using delicatessens!'

The only way to deal with the remark was to treat it seriously. 'What about cassoulet without haricot beans? Milanese sauce without plum tomatoes? How could we manage without good quality rice, pasta, dried fruit, and pulses? Many Indian and Chinese dishes call for special sauces that the ordinary cook would find far too difficult and time-consuming to prepare. We're all getting more and more interested in cooking ethnic dishes and rely on firms such as Finer Foods to provide us with such essential items as poppadoms, sesame-seed oil, and soy sauce. And as a cook I'm just as grateful as you to have a good source of ready prepared foods. I keep certain tins in my store cupboard for emergencies, unexpected guests, when I want to save time or haven't the energy for poaching fruit, or cooking vegetables for a salad or to go in a sauce. There are lots and lots of uses for the top-quality products Finer Foods market.' Darina stopped suddenly. She was getting carried away again.

Joyce Pigram looked stunned. 'I can't say I'd ever thought of it like that,' she said faintly.

William laughed. 'Darina loves talking about food, be warned, Ma dear!'

'I'm sorry,' Darina apologized, 'I'll try not to do it again.'

'I love your enthusiasm,' John Pigram said, starting to clear away the plates.

'What are you doing, darling?'

'Starting our partnership, my dear. I think William's quite right, the woman shouldn't be lumbered with all the boring housework.'

'Well, just don't drop anything.'

Chapter Fifteen

Late Tuesday morning Peter Drax said goodbye to a patient's wife and walked down the path to his car. His mind was not on the case of flu he had just left, yet another to add to the growing total in the district, it was replaying the scene he'd had with Fiona at breakfast.

The post had brought several bills. He'd opened the last, for an extravagantly expensive exercise cycle he had forgotten he'd ordered, and realized she was talking about Christmas; presents for the children, presents for the relations, the party they usually gave. A cash register in his mind started ringing up totals and he stopped her in mid-flight.

'Forget about a party this year.'

She sat gaping at him, a pretty woman in a fluffy angora sweater that had cost over £200. He knew because that was another of the bills he had just opened.

'And we must cut down on presents, including those for the kids.'

There had followed a list of exactly what their son and daughter were expecting to receive, details of how upset they were going to be if any of it was not forthcoming, plus enquiries about the skiing holiday she said he'd promised to take her on after the children went back to school.

'Look,' he'd grated at her. 'There isn't the money, so just forget it, right?'

He'd gulped his coffee, picked up his bag, and left the house with her sitting at the table looking at the debris of breakfast, the mail, and her life.

He'd had a pang of conscience on his way to the surgery. It wasn't his wife's fault she wasn't the brightest of people and he couldn't say he didn't know that when he married her.

He'd wanted Fiona from the first time he set eyes on her. It had been at a pre-Christmas party and she'd worn something silvery that slithered and shimmered around her pretty, plump body. A *diamanté* clasp held back waves of curly black hair. Her mouth was pink and soft, a rosebud of a mouth. Her eyes, brilliant green, the eyes of the medical school cat, flirted with every man who approached. He'd been instantly jealous of them all and moved in swiftly, monopolizing her for the rest of the evening. He'd taken her home, extracted her telephone number, and claimed kisses at the door of her flat after she had refused him coffee. Kisses that started soft and sweet and escalated dangerously quickly into body-churning intensity. Until, like an oiled eel, she'd slipped out of his arms, said a breathless goodnight, and disappeared inside.

He laid siege to her, ringing her at every opportunity. He rang her flat, seldom finding her in, and the office where she worked, receptionist to a firm of advertising agents. She would squeal with horror at his voice on the office phone and complain clients wouldn't be able to get through, promising to go out with him, she claimed, just to get him off the line. When he had managed to get his studying done he couldn't now understand.

Anna and his mother had been unable to comprehend his fixation. That was what they had called it; not love, not passion, a fixation. 'She's such a stupid little girl,' Anna, his overbearing elder sister, had said. 'What on earth will you talk about? You can't spend the whole time in bed!'

His mother had been more tactful. 'Do be very certain what you need out of marriage, my darling,' she'd counselled.

But he'd known what she meant. 'I suppose you married Joel for his conversation,' he'd taunted her.

She'd flushed but stood her ground. 'Partly, yes, I did. He makes me laugh. That's very important.'

'I remember you telling Dad to be serious, stop fooling about; you didn't want to do much laughing with *him*! One law for one and one for another. Well, you're not laying down the law to me.' He'd stalked out, bitterly hurt at yet more proof she was totally unable to understand him and retreated into his magic new world with Fiona.

They'd got married, he had qualified then applied for a short-service commission. He was posted to Germany, as he had hoped. Anything to get away from the family. From his mother, so wrapped up in her company and her toyboy, from Anna's taunts, and from the way Fiona looked at Joel when she thought her husband's attention was elsewhere.

He couldn't claim the move had been a success. Indeed, it had nearly ended in disaster. But they had survived.

Out of the Army again, he'd found a partnership, uncomfortably near home but it was definitely the best thing on offer at the time and his mother had seemed happy to have him back. Relations all round, in fact, were easier. Anna was married, her attentions focused on Charles and her fashion career, and Fiona was pregnant with their first child. It was obvious to Peter that she would now settle down and become a proper wife and mother.

They bought a nice house. Fiona said they couldn't possibly live in it as it was so they spent a fortune on modernizing, decorating, and furnishing their home sweet home. He hadn't worried. The income from his Finer Foods shares was decent, he'd inherited some capital from his grandfather, and his GP earnings weren't exactly on the poverty line. He told Fiona to order what she wanted.

It became the pattern for their marriage. She ordered and he paid.

Over the years he'd sold this investment and that to cover the odd shortfall in income. Finer Foods was doing well and expanding all the time, and when the children's education was finished he could replace the capital out of income, or so he told himself.

But there were still several years of education to come, his capital was exhausted, and the company dividends were sharply down.

Why couldn't Marian have left her estate to him instead of to Anna? He had just as much right to it as his sister. Just because Fiona had never made much effort to be nice to her ('Your aunt's such a bore,' she always said when he asked if they could have her round), didn't mean he hadn't been fond of her. Always gave her a good present at Christmas. Well, he asked Fiona to get her something nice and it wasn't his fault if she didn't have the knack of choosing suitable gifts. He had a sudden vision of his aunt's face last year as she opened an expensive lingerie box to find a Viyella nightie, voluminous, warm, and sexless. They'd been gathered round his mother's Christmas tree, it had been the last of her traditional festive days, already he could see the end in her skeletal figure and pain-drugged eyes but she had, as always, put on a tremendous show.

103

Joel had teased Marian. 'A real man-grabber that one,' he'd said. Everyone had laughed but his aunt had flushed painfully. When Peter had complained to Fiona afterwards about the unsuitability of the gift, she became aggrieved. 'After all,' she said in that unattractive whine she developed when he dared to criticize her in any way, 'it's not as though she's a teenager. I thought she'd like something to keep her warm, it was terribly expensive.' What had mainly worried him though was the look he had caught Fiona giving Joel at the time that had hinted at some secret understanding. He hadn't said anything but it had started him checking up on her in a way he had given up years ago.

Peter Drax got in his car, confirmed that he'd paid the last patient call on his morning list, and started the engine of his Jaguar XJS. There would just be time for a chat with Joel. He had to be made to see that if the company profits continued declining in this way they'd all be in a pretty state.

Maggie, the attractive Finer Foods receptionist, who always made him feel he still had something going for him despite a receding hair line, said Joel was expected back shortly.

Peter went to wait in the Managing Director's office. There he found Michael Berkeley. Peter liked the Sales Director. Michael had taken him to one or two interesting clubs, he was quite sophisticated despite that desperately suburban wife of his, and they always had a good time. Michael told him things he said he'd never told anyone. Including details he'd learned about the Drax family over the years. Peter stored most of these away for future use and discovered the Sales Director seldom remembered anything of their conversations.

Michael tapped a sheaf of papers he'd laid on Joel's desk and announced that the latest sales figures were quite encouraging. Peter said he was pleased to hear it.

'Thought it would improve the day for you. Though good sales figures don't necessarily mean improved profits, as we're all discovering. It's a bit of a mystery to me where the money's all going, and now poor Marian's dead, it's going to be even more difficult to find out. But don't let's be too pessimistic. We haven't had an evening out for several weeks, have we, Doc? Time we found a spot of trouble for ourselves, don't you think?'

Right, said Peter, but he was rather busy just now. He'd give Michael a ring when he was free. He watched the Sales Director go with mingled relief and regret. But the last thing he needed at the moment was an expensive night's gambling, and his luck never seemed any better than Michael's.

He opened Joel's fridge; for a host who hardly drank it was always generously loaded with everything anyone might like for a pre-lunch aperitif, not to mention what the Managing Director referred to as his essential medication.

Twenty minutes later, Peter put down his glass of whisky, decided Joel wasn't coming back before lunch, and went in search of his sister.

Anna was in her office, contemplating some packaging mock-ups sitting in solitary splendour on the polished surface of her desk.

'Look at these,' she said. 'I've been working on them for months.'

Peter looked. Labels with an unfamiliar brand name identified lychees, bean sprouts, water chestnuts, and sesame oil. The packaging was stylish with Oriental lettering.

'This,' said his sister, 'is a small range of specialist Oriental foods I've interested one of the supermarkets in.' She gloated over the mock-ups – there was no other word to describe her expression of proud possession.

'So?'

Irritation, so familiar from their childhood confrontations, crossed her face. 'You always have to have everything spelled out, don't you, Peter? Well, this could be just what we need. Strong representation in the supermarkets without upsetting the delicatessen trade. Finer Foods will never be mentioned, it will appear a totally new brand.'

'What does Joel say?'

'Is that all you're interested in? What Joel will say?' Her voice mimicked his with savage cruelty.

'I'm interested in the profitability of this company,' he said with as much dignity as he could muster.

'Well, little brother, Joel will object because of the cost, as I suppose you will too. It will require a substantial investment. There's palleting as well as packaging. And we have to commit ourselves to a large initial consignment. Supermarkets set stringent conditions on quality, quantities, packaging, delivery, and there's no compromising. If you want their business, you have to meet their requirements.'

'But you reckon it's worth it?'

'Sure! If this line goes down as well as I, and they, expect, it will be big business. But all Joel will see is that the company can't afford both this' – she waved a hand at the collection on her desk – 'and this ridiculous idea of opening our own chain of delicatessens.'

'Is it? Ridiculous?'

'You have no idea about any aspect of this business, have you, brother dear? A delicatessen will call for sizeable initial capital, require constant supervision, and would be an investment in a fading past. Delicatessens and specialist grocers have no future. Oh, a few might keep going, in high-spending areas with exclusive tastes; for the rest of the country, ninety-nine per cent of the population will shop at supermarkets. My daughters might just have sufficient incentive to spend time searching out and visiting specialist shops, their friends probably won't have the time and certainly not the inclination. One-stop shopping is what they are into. And modern supermarkets like Sainsbury and Safeway cater for them. They bake bread, have wet fish and delicatessen counters, and stock items that are a far cry from the pile it high and sell it cheap days.'

His sister could be very persuasive when she wanted to be, Peter thought. He had a quick mental vision of her specialist range of Oriental foods in thousands of check-out baskets in supermarkets all over the country. With a good profit margin built in, those products could transform the Finer Foods dividend.

How long was it going to take to cover the costs and start making money? he asked Anna.

'That's all you're really interested in, isn't it? Quick returns. If Joel told you his delicatessen scheme would bring instant money, you'd be all for that, wouldn't you?'

He tried to explain his cash-flow problem with the downturn in the company profits. 'After all, sis, your income must be hurting as well. I know Johnson pays for the girls' schooling but there's that au pair you call a housekeeper, you've got an expensive house and car, and,' he said, eyeing her chic two-piece, 'you must spend just as much on your clothes as Fiona does.'

But instead of agreeing times were difficult, Anna launched into a personal attack, accused him of being a parasite that lived on other's people's efforts, said Fiona was a clothes horse who knew nothing about reality, that it would do them both good to have to cut down a bit, and called the children spoilt brats who would come to no harm if their ridiculous demands weren't met every once in a while. Then she paused, shot him a calculating glance, and added, 'Peter, as long as Joel is at the helm you needn't look to this company for income. I can only see things getting worse.'

He looked at her in alarm.

'Why don't you come in with me? If both of us joined forces with Michael, we'd outnumber Joel's shares and could vote him off the board. I could take over the company and then things would really start moving.'

Peter sat himself down in a chair by her desk and stared at his sister but he couldn't say the suggestion came as a total surprise. Anna had got him together with Marian as soon as their mother's will was known. She had been terrifyingly angry, angrier than he had ever known her, which was saying something.

What about Michael Berkeley? Marian had asked. Anna had swept the query aside saying Marian knew as well as she that if they all agreed Michael would go along with them, that he liked Joel no more than they did.

Peter knew immediately Anna had made a bad mistake. Marian wasn't what you could call a strong character or particularly intelligent but, when she wanted to, she could dig her heels in. Anna might dislike Joel, she didn't. Peter couldn't understand how Anna had missed that.

But she had never been a particularly good judge of character. She had adored their father, always believed him when he said it was Eleanor's fault none of his schemes came to anything. If she could only be a better wife, he said, be there for him instead of spending all her time on her own little ploys, he'd be able to make something of himself. He completely ignored the fact that if it weren't for Eleanor's money and 'little ploys' the family would find life extremely difficult. But Peter and Anna had both resented their mother's frequent absences, her absorption with the company. It had provided a bond between them; when they were married, they would declare to each other, they wouldn't neglect their families. Then they would fall to fighting about something else.

What was so ironic now was that Anna had neglected her marriage and children as comprehensively as her mother had. If only Peter could be certain she was as good a businesswoman as Eleanor.

Surely if she was she would have been made deputy Managing Director and it would have been her who received those vital shares when her mother died, not Joel? And it had to be admitted, however much you loathed the man's morals, he had managed his own very successful business, even if it had been in fashion rather than food. Anna had never made it beyond junior management until she joined Finer Foods and Peter couldn't see that she'd done anything particularly noteworthy since then.

Her first bid to out-vote Joel had ended in Marian's gentle but total refusal to join in. Relieved at having had the decision taken out of his hands, Peter managed to escape from the meeting without openly defying his furious sister. Now he was going to have to commit himself one way or the other.

'Sorry,' he said at last. 'I think Joel's a better bet for looking after my interests than you would be.' He flipped a finger at one of the mock-ups, knocking it over. 'And I don't give much for your chances at getting this lot on the supermarket shelves either.'

He rose and left the office before Anna could return to the attack.

He picked up a sandwich for lunch then drove back to the surgery totting up expenditure and setting against the total such income as he could count on. The shortfall was more than alarming, it was disastrous.

Chapter Sixteen

The following afternoon Darina arrived at Finer Foods. Her book was not going well. She had amassed a great deal of information on the products, noted down a number of recipes that could display many of them to good advantage, and had ideas for more, but lacked what she thought of as a 'unifying image' to pull it all together and give the book a thrust that would fire the imagination of potential readers.

So she abandoned her notes and her word processor and decided what she needed was a talk with Joel Madoc.

When she arrived at his office, Finer Foods' managing director did not look well. His eyes were too bright, his face was flushed, and when he tried to discuss the book with Darina he seemed unable to concentrate.

'Don't worry,' she said when he apologized. 'Why don't we leave it? You look as though you're coming down with this flu that's about, you really ought to go home, go to bed.' Darina started to gather together the notes and recipes she'd laid out on the coffee table in his office.

Joel straightened his back. 'Nonsense, I'm fine, just a bit tired. Had Peter on my back this morning, he popped into the office between patients to bend my ear about the necessity for getting the dividend up. That boy's getting above himself, even took a whisky from my fridge without asking. I told him he'd better watch it, doctors with alcohol on their breath start losing their practices; if that happened, he really would be in trouble. Anyway, there's no point in going home, Jane's away for a couple of days and I'd only have to cook my own supper.'

'Come and eat with us,' Darina heard herself say. 'With any luck William should be home at a reasonable hour tonight.'

'Great.' Joel jumped up as though he'd received an injection of new energy. 'We can continue our discussion then. All I need is a good meal and I'll be back on top form.'

Darina gave instructions on how to find the cottage and drove home planning what she would serve for supper. In the fridge were some Swedish salted herrings Finer Foods imported that she had prepared in various sauces the other day. They would do for a first course.

There was a batch of her puff pastry in the deep-freeze. If the butcher had fillet steak, she could produce individual boeuf en croute, easy to pop in the oven with no last-minute attention at the stove needed.

She stopped off and bought rye bread and the meat and found mange tout at the greengrocer. She added sour cream for baked potatoes to her purchases and set off for home thinking zabaglione would be fun for pudding. Joel liked Italian food and they would be eating in the kitchen so she could easily whisk it up while the men ate some cheese. And there was just time to make some langues de chat biscuits.

The evening was a disaster.

William opened the door to Joel and took him through to the living room.

'I think your friend is drunk,' he hissed to Darina as he searched in the freezer compartment for some ice. 'Can we eat soon?'

Darina quickly finished her clearing up and went through to join them.

Joel, his face even more flushed than it had been in the afternoon, staggered slightly as he rose to greet her. 'Wonderful to have me.' He spoke with the exaggerated care of the man who has had more to drink than is wise. 'Rescued a lonely man.' He smiled uncertainly at William. 'Lucky chap to have this lovely girl. Intelligent too.'

'And a great cook,' William said heartily, 'as we are about to discover, aren't we?'

Darina took them through to the kitchen. But Joel had to disappear before joining them at the table.

'I'm sorry,' Darina hissed at her fiancé, 'I don't know what's happened. I've never seen him like this before.'

Somehow they got through the meal, Joel extravagantly praising the food.

'Don't feel you've got to eat it,' Darina said as he seemed to be having difficulty with the pastry round the meat. She never knew how to make guests realize it wouldn't upset her if they left something on their plates, they seemed to feel it would be a mortal insult not to down everything and ask for more.

Small talk having been exhausted at the cheese stage, William turned to asking about business.

Joel gave them a long-winded story of some disastrous consignment from Hong Kong.

'Is the labels, you see,' he said, sounding drunker than ever. He had refused alcohol since his arrival but the food hadn't helped to produce any sobering effect. 'The labels are orl right, qui' orl right. At least, thass what they look like. Look like the real thing. Yes, the real thing, thass it. But it isn't.'

'Isn't what?' asked William patiently as Darina put the bowl containing the egg yolks, Marsala, and sugar on a pan of simmering water and started to whisk.

'Isn't right. Isn't the real thing.'

'You mean the labels aren't?'

'Ah!' Joel leaned forward and William swiftly fielded the wine bottle. 'Thass the question, see? Are the labels the real thing or not?' He considered it for a moment. 'But it doesn't really matter because the tins aren't.'

'Ah, I think I've got it. You've had a consignment of goods that look as though they are what you ordered but when you open them, the contents are not what you expected?' Darina thought William some sort of genius to have sorted that out from Joel's ramblings.

'Din't I juss say that? Well, right, thass it!'

'What's wrong with the contents?' Darina felt she should play her part. After all, it was she who had invited Joel here. She wondered if he went on a binge often.

He swivelled heavily in his chair to face her as she stood whisking at the stove. 'In-fer-i-or,' he said carefully, dragging out each syllable. 'Can't sell them. Trouble is, trouble is,' he faltered, looked vaguely around the kitchen for help, then seemed to gather his slipping wits together. 'We've paid for the buggers. By letter of credit.'

'Which means?'

'Letter of credit is non-cancellable,' said William. 'Joel means the company has bought a load of duff stock and may not be able to get its money back.'

'But surely you can complain to the suppliers?' Darina ladled ribbons of aromatic yellow foam into glasses and put them on the table, wondering if Marsala-laden zabaglione was such a good idea after all.

Joel gazed at it with joy. 'Juss like mama use make,' he

breathed. Darina handed him the plate of langues de chat. He took several. 'Shou'n't, of course, specially after pastry,' he mumbled, spitting out crumbs of the light biscuits, 'but been such a goo' boy, lil treat won't hurt.'

Darina gave up any idea of pursuing the business of the faulty Finer Foods consignment, finished her dessert and made coffee.

She kept filling Joel's cup with the strong black liquid as they sat again in the living room but it had little effect. Attempts at conversation were finally abandoned in favour of the news on television. At the end of the broadcast, William switched off and turned to their guest. He appeared to have gone to sleep.

'Oh God,' he said. 'Do we call a taxi or put him up for the night?'

Darina could hear just how reluctant he was to have Joel on the premises a moment longer than necessary. But they couldn't put him in a taxi in that condition, what would happen at the other end? 'I'll find the sheets,' she said.

Their spare room was tiny and didn't offer much manoeuvring room for putting drunken men to bed. It was just as well William was tall and strong for there was no space for Darina to help him once they were upstairs. He levered Joel on to the bed with difficulty, the effort bringing him down almost on top of the comatose man. Joel's mouth fell open and William involuntarily jerked his head back, then he disentangled himself from the unconscious form, bent towards the man's face again, and inhaled with the care of a vintner assessing a wine's credentials.

'Come here and take a sniff.' William stepped back from the bed to allow Darina to squeeze alongside. 'What does that smell like to you?'

With a good deal of reluctance – she disliked alcohol-laden breath – Darina did as she was asked. 'Nail-varnish remover!' she exclaimed in surprise.

William felt in Joel's pockets, then investigated the one inside his jacket. He took out a small leather case and unfastened it. 'I thought so!' He showed Darina an orange-topped syringe and two small bottles. 'Insulin, the man's diabetic. We were wrong in thinking he was drunk, this is a coma!'

He took out the syringe, filled it from one of the bottles, then ripped down Joel's trousers, exposing his thighs, disfigured with scarring. He plunged in the needle, finished the injection, then stood back.

'I've used the quick-acting insulin and I hope that'll do the trick but we'd better call an ambulance.'

Darina stood waiting for her emergency call to be answered, her mind reeling. Joel a diabetic? It seemed so strange, he hadn't shown any signs. Then she asked herself impatiently why he should. Apart from the need to inject themselves, most diabetics led normal lives. Then she remembered that they also needed to watch what they ate. Had his collapse been something to do with the meal she had given him? She didn't think he was the sort of man to forget his vital shots of insulin.

Back upstairs after giving the ambulance service the full details, she found the situation unchanged. 'Why hasn't he responded?' she asked William.

'I don't know,' he said slowly. 'But the fact that he hasn't is serious, very serious.'

Darina looked at her fiancé's concerned face and then at the unconscious man. She felt a deep sense of unease. First Marian Drax had been murdered and now Joel appeared to be slipping deeper and deeper into unconsciousness.

Chapter Seventeen

Darina and William followed the ambulance to hospital. By the time they parked the car, Joel had been whisked away and a doctor was waiting to speak to them. He looked grave and was uncommunicative, took the insulin kit William had found in Joel's pocket and wanted to know what the patient had eaten and whether he had been neglecting his injections. William explained the situation, including how he had injected their comatose guest. Once the doctor realized they had no further information, he told them they could continue to wait if they wanted to and disappeared.

'I feel like an unexpected guest who's told he can stay for dinner but only if he sticks to the salad,' complained Darina as they sat down once again in the waiting area of the casualty department. 'Do you think anybody will bother to tell us what's happening with Joel? Don't they realize how worried we are?'

A green-clad orderly wheeled an empty gurney along the wide corridor behind the chairs. An Anglepoise lamp lit the desk of the receiving nurse and left the rest of the area around her in shadow. The ceiling lights above the waiting area had been dimmed to a level that seemed designed to encourage somnolence. At the far end of a row of chairs a girl in her twenties sat with a man's anorak on her lap. There was blood on the anorak and her face was set in lines that acknowledged the brief brutality that could be life.

Darina paced up and down the lines of chairs, her hands pushed deep into the pockets of the bright pink baggy silk trousers she was wearing. She could concentrate on nothing beyond the vision she carried of Joel's unconscious face. Finer Foods had been deprived of its financial director, was it also now to lose its managing director? Nobody had offered an encouraging word since they had arrived and she wasn't cheered by the look of quiet concentration on her fiancé's face.

Abruptly she stopped her pacing and went and sat beside him, slipping a hand through his arm. 'How did you know about insulin and how to inject?'

'It was all part of a St John's Ambulance course I once did.' William took her hand in his, interlacing their fingers in a warm grasp. 'And I had a friend at university who was a diabetic. He had several blackouts but they didn't seem anything like your friend's. He'd start to sweat profusely and his pulse would race. Sometimes he'd get confused or become very aggressive. All through an over-supply of insulin in his blood, usually because he'd played a hard game of rugger. Diabetics aren't able to process sugar without injecting insulin, but not enough food, or a sudden increase in the metabolic rate through a burst of activity like playing rugby, allows a build-up of more insulin than the body can handle. If we caught the situation in time, all that was needed was a couple of sugar lumps or some sweet biscuits and that adjusted the balance. But he was a bit of an idiot and sometimes he got so wrapped up in his work, he forgot to eat, ignored the warning signs, and just passed out. Then he had to have glucose injections.'

'But Joel had just had an enormous meal and you can't say he'd been overactive, not after he'd arrived with us, anyway.'

'I know, I think his trouble is hyper- rather than hypo-glycaemia.'

'What's the difference?'

'Hypo results from too much insulin, like my university friend. Hyper is too little. That's why the doctor wanted to know if Joel had been neglecting his injections. If the body is deprived of insulin, sugar builds up and, again, the body can't cope. Sugar sounds much less of a problem than insulin but I believe hyperglycaemia is the more dangerous condition.'

'What's the treatment?'

'Quite simple, really, insulin.'

Darina felt confused. 'But you injected Joel with insulin.'

'I injected him with what I found in his pocket,' corrected William.

She sat and stared at him.

'Jane is away,' she said at last. 'If he hadn't come round for dinner with us he would have been on his own.'

'Does someone come in in the mornings?' asked William.

'No idea. But if he's in a critical state now, what would the chances be if he hadn't received any attention for eight or nine hours?'

It was a question that didn't need an answer.

After a moment Darina asked, 'What do you think's the matter with the insulin kit you found?'

'My guess is that the bottles have been filled with water, one probably doctored with salt to make it look cloudy.'

It all fitted in.

'Are you going to inform Wiltshire police?'

'I shall ring Chief Inspector Melville in the morning.'

Darina shivered. By then there could be two murders to be investigated. 'This puts a whole new complexion on the Marian Drax case, doesn't it?'

'Doesn't it just!'

'You know there was a power failure the morning she was killed?' Darina heard once again Maggie's screech of complaint as she lost her word-processing program, the second time that morning, she'd said. And the first time the electricity had been off for twenty minutes.

She told William the details. 'So if Joel did his washing up during that twenty minutes, he'd have been safe,' she finished.

'You mean, if the trap had been set for him? You're suggesting the sinks were already electrified when he started his cooking. Who was in the kitchen before him?'

Darina sighed. 'A group of secretaries uses it every morning for breakfast. Finer Foods are thinking of selling a version of those partly-baked croissants that are on the market and they come in early to try them out. They were just finishing clearing up when Joel went in for his session.'

'Just one or two of them?'

'No.' Darina was thinking carefully. 'I gathered the whole lot were there, about six or seven I think. You know, Joel's not at all unpopular amongst the staff in general, just the executives. I don't see them setting that trap as a group.'

'But if Joel actually was the intended victim, who do you suggest could have managed to electrify the sinks? There doesn't seem to be an opportunity for anybody else to get into the kitchen.'

William had merely articulated the problem that had faced Darina as soon as she produced her new theory.

Then they both rose as the doctor who had talked to them earlier came back into the casualty waiting area.

Burdened with a half-bottle of champagne and some light reading matter, Darina turned up at the hospital late the next morning.

A telephone call had established that Joel Madoc was resting comfortably in a private room and visitors were welcome at any time.

At first glance he looked almost his old self and he gave Darina a broad grin as she entered. A second look revealed that the extra-bright eyes were strained and slightly sunken, the skin around them fine drawn with an air of transparency. And once the grin had faded, the mouth was tense.

Darina ignored the hand held out to her, swiftly kissed his cheek, and placed the champagne on the cabinet beside his bed. 'For strength,' she said and handed over a couple of magazines. 'To distract you.' She found a chair, brought it up beside the bed and sat down, thinking how strange it was to be in a hospital room that wasn't decorated with get well cards and bowls of flowers.

'I think I have you and your fiancé to thank for saving my life,' Joel said quietly.

'Have you found out what happened yet?'

It was as William had supposed, they thought his insulin had been replaced with water. 'It's got to be tested properly but they are pretty certain I'd been without insulin for nearly thirty-six hours. I took those bottles from the fridge before I left the office the day before yesterday; my other lot had run out and I wasn't going home before picking up Jane for an evening out. I remember thinking it was a little odd the seals had gone from their tops, I hadn't remembered taking them off when I put the bottles in the office fridge. I always keep some there, ready for when the others run out.'

'How long had they been there?'

'Those bottles? Oh, not more than a few days.'

He was talking too much, Darina thought. She watched his hands smoothing the top of the sheet, picking at the blanket.

'I'm afraid, though, the collapse last night was partly my fault. I should have realized I was going into a hyperglycaemic condition; as it was, I just assumed it was the flu, half the office seems to have come down with a case and I knew I had had my injections, you see. The last thing I should have done was eat all that delicious food you gave me, far too much carbohydrate, alas. Even if I'd been completely fit, I should have picked and chosen better but as it was I behaved like a pig and paid the price, it accelerated the collapse.'

The charm with which he said it was almost irresistible. The

117

white of the bed linen played up the grey in his hair and the golden tones of his tanned skin. No wonder the nurses fell in love with patients.

'How long will you have to stay here?'

'They've got my metabolism readjusted already and I may be able to leave this afternoon, they just wanted to be sure I'm really not coming down with flu, but I know I'm not. Can't wait to get out of here. I phoned the office and told them I wouldn't be in until tomorrow.' He laughed. 'Bit of a shock for them, hearing I was in hospital!'

'Does everyone there know you are a diabetic?'

'I've never made any secret of it. There's always insulin in my office fridge and I shouldn't think my midday tryst with the executive loo for the pre-lunch jab has gone unnoticed. You learn the hard way to treat it all as normal.'

His voice was light but flavoured with a bitterness that was revealing. Darina asked how long he had been a diabetic.

'About seventeen years. At least, that's the length of time it's been diagnosed.' He was back to smoothing the sheet again. Darina let the little silence lengthen. 'I met Eleanor just after that.' He looked from her towards the window where curtains in large checks framed a view on to another hospital ward. 'Anna and I had been seeing something of each other.' He paused briefly. 'She was – is – very attractive and there was something different about her. She asked me down to her home to meet her mother, just after the doctor had told me the results of the tests. It was the most shattering thing that had happened to me.'

He smiled at Darina, an ironic, rueful smile. 'My life up till then had been a success story. Everything I'd wanted, I'd had. My company was doing very well, I had a new girlfriend, a smart flat, a fast car, I was the golden boy. Then, wham, out of nowhere, this. Not quite out of nowhere, of course. I wouldn't have been at the doctor's if I hadn't known something was wrong. But I was so confident, sure he'd say, sorry, it's got to be an operation, or a course of treatment, but then you'll be one hundred per cent again. It was going to a minor blip in my upward progress on the primrose path to comprehensive happiness. Instead he gave me a lifetime's sentence. A lifetime of injecting myself three times a day. I tell you, the golden boy didn't take it at all well.'

'How did Anna take the news?' Darina asked after a moment. 'I suppose you told her?'

The rueful smile was back. 'I told her in the car on the way down. I think I was treating it as my test on how the world was going to react. If she said it wasn't important, just a small nuisance, then I could treat it that way as well.'

'I take it she didn't react well.'

'Understatement of the year,' said Joel. 'Oh, looking back, I can understand. She was very young, in her early twenties, I was over thirty. I learned later that she had worshipped her father, who'd died a few years earlier. I think she'd built me up in her mind into some sort of superhero father-substitute, a role that until that point I no doubt fulfilled rather successfully. Then she was suddenly told her superman had some disgusting sounding illness that meant he'd become a junkie – not only that, he was never going to get better.' Joel's voice was full of scorn, not for Anna but for the position in which he had put her, for the false impression he'd had of life and his place in it. Darina could see exactly the sort of young man he'd been.

'So we arrived at her mother's house with both of us in a state of shock. The moment we got there, Anna just melted away, leaving Eleanor with this unknown young man to cope with.' He smiled reminiscently. 'She was wonderful. It didn't take long before I was telling her about the diabetes and she was reassuring me that I would get used to it all in no time and it wouldn't really make any difference. And she made me realize there were so many worse things I could be suffering from. Like, for instance, the cancer that killed her. She even asked if I needed any help with the injections because I'd told her what a blue funk I was in before the first one. And it wasn't long before we were laughing together and the whole thing had been placed in proportion as far as I was concerned. I was just so grateful to her.

'Anna and I went out once or twice after that but the magic had gone. I found myself organizing a shirt promotion in a store not far from here and asking Eleanor out to dinner. After that one thing led to another.'

'She sounds a very attractive woman, I'm sorry I never met her.'

'Oh, you would have liked her so much, and she would have loved meeting you, you could have talked food together for ever. I think she was always disappointed Anna wasn't more interested, it was one of a series of small difficulties between them. I think Eleanor knew more about food than anyone I've ever met. Even Jane.' He looked at Darina. 'I've been so lucky, to have found two such women as Eleanor and Jane.'

'What a pity,' said Darina, 'that Jane had to go away.'

Joel looked gloomy. 'Isn't it? I could really do with her now.' Then he looked embarrassed. 'I don't mean I'm not grateful to you but, well . . .'

'I know what you mean. I'd hate to be ill and not have William to hold my hand.'

'Your poor fiancé, what must he have thought about my behaviour last night! As soon as he's got a free evening, we'll take you both out to dinner.'

'When will Jane be back?'

'I don't know. She received some sort of message yesterday morning, an old friend was in trouble and needed her, so off she dashed.'

'Can you ring her and tell her what's happened?'

'Wouldn't dream of it, I'm fine now. Anyway, I haven't got a telephone number. She'll ring me this evening, I'm sure.'

But at that moment Joel's door opened and Jane herself entered with the little rush Darina associated with her.

'Darling! What's been happening?' She flung herself at him but almost immediately disentangled herself and drew back to look at him properly. 'Are you really all right? I set off terribly early this morning, rang you from the shop as soon as I arrived, only to be told you'd been brought in here!' Little gasps interrupted every phrase and it took some time for Joel to assure her that he really was fine. Finally she took in what had happened.

She sat down heavily in the chair Darina had given her, shock widening her eyes. There were puffy bags beneath them and their usually bright blue was faded and strained, the whites unattractively marbled with red veining; for a moment she looked quite plain and very ordinary.

Darina got in a quick goodbye and suggested they once again postpone her visit to Jane's delicatessen, scheduled for the next afternoon.

But Joel insisted he didn't need any looking after and Jane said if she didn't have something to take her mind off everything, she'd probably go round the bend.

'I just don't know what's going on around here,' she said to Joel. 'Do you know Betty never sent that message at all? She said she didn't know why I'd come!'

Chapter Eighteen

Salads offered themselves like jewels under veils: tomatoes, peppers, and beans shining through limpid dressings, pale celery, nuts, and potatoes promising additional texture and flavour.

Darina had gone to visit Jane's delicatessen determined to get to the bottom of how she had been lured away from her fiancé's side, certain only this could throw some light on who had attempted to kill Joel.

She kept going over the account Joel had given her of the insulin he'd kept in his office. He'd said the bottles that had had their contents switched had been there several days. The murderer would have had to check to see when he had begun to use them, otherwise he or she wouldn't have known when to send Jane that false message. But checking wouldn't have been difficult, too many people had access to Joel's office. It would only have taken a moment to open the fridge door and look at the bottles.

Darina felt frustrated by both too little and too much information. Anna Drax Johnson, Michael Berkeley, and Peter Drax had all had access to the fridge for switching the liquid in the bottles. Joel had said Peter had visited his office the morning of his collapse and had helped himself to a drink. A call to Maggie had established the doctor had spent nearly half an hour alone in there the day before. But was a drop in the dividend enough to stimulate him to kill the Managing Director? Anna and Michael were more obvious suspects, either could have expected to take over the company themselves, and both were constantly in and out of the managing director's office; switching the insulin and checking the bottles would have been child's play.

But motive or no, all of them had water-tight alibis for the attempt that had killed Marian Drax. And surely the person responsible for the attack on Joel was also responsible for the Financial Director's death?

If only Jane could identify who knew she had a friend some way away from Somerset who could call on her for instant help. If only there was some further information she could supply on Joel and his use of insulin; after all, she was more or less living with him.

Darina's mouth watered as she studied Jane's chilled cabinet display. 'How do you decide on what to offer?' she asked.

'A lot of it has been trial and error. I worked in a delicatessen in south London before I came here and thought how boring their selection was, I was dying to offer something different. But when I started here I had to throw away gallons of exciting concoctions that hadn't sold. Some were too expensive, others too different and some used ingredients you couldn't always guarantee to get hold of; people get really annoyed when they like something and you haven't got it when they want it. So I've learned to temper my enthusiasms. After all, it won't help my customers if I go out of business.'

Darina moved on to look at the selection of cold meats: pale pink hams, roast beef with rich brown crust and rosily underdone centre, pork with its subtle richness. 'Do you cook the joints yourself?'

'Oh, yes. I have an automatic boiler for the hams. I get them from a local supplier, mostly already boned. They're vacuum-packed and I cook them like that, then all the juices remain wrapped round the meat. In the summer we get through about forty a week, at this time of the year about half that but demand goes up again at Christmas. I get lots of orders for whole hams then, finished in the oven with brown sugar and cider.'

'Hams are not what they used to be,' Darina sighed. 'They aren't cured, merely injected with brine. The flesh is wringing wet and there's no flavour. Yours, of course,' she added hastily, 'look far better than that. But I bet they don't have the taste of a properly cured ham.'

'No,' acknowledged Jane, 'but they are a good deal cheaper. I offer York ham that's been properly dry cured at Christmas but at other times of the year I would throw away more than I sold. And you can't really blame the customers, half of them don't know any better and many have to watch the pennies so carefully. They look at the price, not the quality. But I always insist on roasting the meats properly.'

'What do you mean?' Darina was fascinated by this glimpse into the hazards of selling fresh food.

'There are retailers who will stoop to anything to cut a few pence off what they offer, or to maximize their profits. Like, for instance, boiling joints then giving them a quick ten minutes in the oven right at the end.'

'So they don't lose all the weight that disappears when you roast properly?'

'Right. Something between thirty and forty per cent is lost in the oven, that can make quite a difference to your economics per slice.'

Surrounded by the tangible evidence of her hard work and success, Jane Leslie lost the suggestion of helpless little woman she wore around Joel. Her manner was crisp and decided. As she showed Darina around, her eyes never stopped assessing what was happening in the shop. She would interrupt an explanation of some point to dart away and rearrange a display shelf or quietly help a customer having difficulty finding what she wanted. Her staff seemed to know exactly what they were doing and Darina admired the spirit of cheerful camaraderie that there seemed to be not only amongst themselves but also in their relationship with the proprietor. Jane Leslie ran an impressive operation and Darina found her initial assessment of her undergoing a change.

'Come and have a cup of tea,' Jane offered. 'I've got a new cheesecake I want to try. We can have a nice chat away from the hurly-burly.'

She led Darina through a door at the side of the shop to a stairway that wound up to the owner's quarters on the first floor and into a nicely proportioned room. Then she disappeared, refusing help, saying she'd bring the tea through in a minute.

So Darina went over to the window and looked out on to the busy little main street where the delicatessen rubbed shoulders with a gentlemen's outfitters and an old-fashioned hardware store. Across the road was a greengrocer's, the pavement lined with well-stacked trestles of fast-moving produce, and a butcher's, the window filled with superior-looking chickens. Inside Darina could see a queue of people waiting their turn to be served. Not everyone did their shopping in the mornings, it seemed. The activity was beginning to tail off now the afternoon was more than half-way through but there were still enough customers around to make any storekeeper's heart glad.

It seemed Jane Leslie had found herself a good site in a promising catchment area. 'I wanted somewhere that didn't offer supermarket competition,' she had told Darina. 'And a business I could build up. This seemed ideal.'

Jane reappeared with the tea, fragrant Darjeeling, and a good-looking cheesecake of the cooked variety. Darina looked at the slice, beautifully studded with raisins, and asked where Jane found her freshly cooked produce. There was no way she had the time to prepare it herself.

'It's getting more and more difficult with the new regulations. So much fresh food has to be kept below a certain temperature all the way from preparation through delivery to the store and display to actual sale. That means refrigerated delivery vans as well as chilled display cabinets. One firm who used to do marvellous quiches and pies now only do cakes and sweet things like treacle tarts that fall outside the temperature regulations. And I can't get frozen goat's milk from another supplier because it isn't worth her while to buy a refrigerated van for the five minutes it takes to deliver it here. So I've lost another source. This cheesecake is from a company that started up recently, I shudder to think of the investment they must have made to conform to all the hygiene and temperature regulations. Let's try it.' She dug a fork into the creamy slice and ate a piece.

Darina told herself it was all in the interests of science and wished she didn't put weight on quite so easily. 'How do you keep your figure?' she asked Jane. 'You're about half my size.'

'You can't call me tiny!' Jane gave a squawk of laughter. 'I go on regular deprivation weeks, but if it weren't for all the running around, I'd be a regular butterball. Just as well Joel says he likes women cuddly.'

'How is he?'

'Fine, he's back at work today, behaving as though nothing had happened.'

But of course it had. Jane had given Darina the perfect opening.

'Has he any idea what happened with the insulin?'

Jane's smile died; her face altered, became closed. 'I'd rather not talk about it, if you don't mind.'

'Please, it's very important. Have you any idea who could have sent that message to you?'

'I told you, I don't want to talk about it, and you have no right to ask me.'

Darina could no more pursue the subject than she could have asked the Queen where she bought her underwear. She felt frustrated and puzzled. Why should the topic be so fraught with difficulty for Jane?

'Will you go on running this place after you get married?'

'Of course! I've put far too much into it to give it up just like that. It means too much to me.' There was a note of fierce possession in her voice.

Darina asked about her early struggles. Gradually the woman's face relaxed as she detailed the problems of not being able to afford enough staff, her difficulties with sorting out suppliers and ordering routines, the battle to modernize the shop without disrupting business. 'I've kept a record of everything I've done, with photographs and cuttings.' She rose from her chair, went to a desk, and opened a drawer. 'It should give you a better idea than anything I can tell you.'

Just then one of her assistants popped her head round the door, 'I'm sorry to interrupt but there's a customer with a query, could you come?'

Jane said she'd be down directly then placed a heavy leatherbound volume on the desk. 'Have a look through that, I shouldn't be long.'

The book was labelled *The Delicatessen*. Darina sat at the desk and flipped quickly through it, studying one or two of the before and after photographs with interest and skimming a couple of articles from local journals that hailed a bright newcomer to the Somerset food scene. Then she glanced at the still open drawer and saw there were more cuttings. She lifted them out, shuffling through to see if she could find an interesting enough angle to hang an article on.

When Jane returned, Darina was staring at a cutting from a south London newspaper of some years earlier. She looked up, shock all over her face, and saw that Jane knew exactly what she had been reading.

'Who told you you could read that?' Jane dashed across the room and snatched away the cutting with vicious force. 'How dare you pry into my life? A person is entitled to privacy, whatever she's done!' She crushed the cutting in her hand and stood over Darina shaking with fury.

Which confirmed that, incredible as it seemed, the photograph accompanying the news story Darina had been reading really was

125

of Jane Leslie, even though the caption identified the woman as one Jean Lovell.

Joel's fiancée had once been convicted of manslaughter: had killed her lover with a kitchen knife.

Chapter Nineteen

William pressed a glass of whisky into Darina's hand and made her sit down.

He'd come back from the office to find her going through the fridge with a set face.

After a little he managed to extract the disastrous end to her afternoon. 'There was nothing I could do,' Darina said, 'she hustled me out of there as though I was an untouchable.'

'Perhaps she felt she was the untouchable one.'

Darina sighed. 'I feel as though I've been knocked into some odd sort of shape that I can't recognize as myself. I didn't mean to pry.'

'Of course you didn't.'

'She told me I was a snoop, said I had no right to dig through her things, asked me if I thought I was the police!' Darina ended on a note of outrage.

'Hardly complimentary to us,' William said drily.

'I felt unclean. Because in a way she was right. I hadn't only gone to her shop to discuss food, I wanted to find out more about what had happened to Joel and that insulin. And who knew about her friend. But she wouldn't discuss any of it.'

'And that made you suspicious?'

Darina thought for a moment. 'Not quite, but until that moment Jane Leslie had always seemed such an open person. Then she shut down, turned off any possibility of discussing what had happened; the change was intriguing. I'd already started altering my opinion of her once I saw how efficiently she ran that shop, I'd expected something a little disorganized, even a bit of a mess, and now she seemed to have become even more complex. It was as if you thought you had hold of a rosy apple and suddenly found it was an onion with all sorts of different skins and layers to be peeled away. I suppose if I'm truthful I was looking through those cuttings for something that could throw a little light on her rather than an angle I could use for an article and she was right, I really was prying.'

'We are always having to poke into other people's lives,' William said gently.

'But you're official, a police officer. You have a duty.' Darina was almost crying.

'Darling, you look like a turkey who's just been told the meaning of Christmas, come here.' He pulled her up gently from the chair, wrapping his arms round her, feeling the solidarity of her familiar bones and flesh melt against his. But the usual communication between them was missing. After a minute she gently removed herself to go and trawl through the deep-freeze to liberate some frost-encrusted packet for their supper. Originally, she'd said, she'd intended to buy something from Jane's delicatessen for them to eat but her departure had been too precipitous.

He watched her pick out an unidentifiable lump wrapped in a plastic bag and made a decision. He took the packet out of her hand and returned it to its chilly resting place. 'Come on, I'm taking you out for a meal, you need cheering up.'

He allowed her time to tidy herself and repair the damage to her face, but it wasn't long before they were seated at the table of a local restaurant, Somerset's answer to a French brasserie, a bottle of more than moderate wine on the table, duck à l'orange on the way.

'Feel any better?' he asked.

She nodded but said nothing. He looked at her, sitting quietly across the table, her long fall of cream hair loose the way he liked it, a touch of make-up turning the grey of her eyes to hazel. He looked at this woman he loved so much and saw something in her face he didn't recognize. Ever since they'd met he'd gloried in her quietly confident approach to life, loved to see her wrestle with problems, cope with difficulties. She hadn't always known the answers but she'd always coped straightforwardly, as though she believed that if she just hung in there everything would come right in the end. Now she looked as though some centre of gravity in her world had shifted.

'You're upset about more than that silly woman this afternoon. Tell me, is it my fault, have I been neglecting you because of the new job?'

'No, of course not. You're my rock, my lynch pin.' For a second something in her reached out and made contact with him. Until that moment he hadn't been aware he was holding his breath. He let it out in a long sigh of relief.

'So, what is it?'

'Oh, darling, I just feel the most terrible sense of failure.'

He hooted, an incredulously stunned reaction that seemed the right one because something in her lightened. Not by very much, but he felt he could deal with this.

'OK, why the sense of failure?'

She said nothing, just picked up a knife and started making patterns in the tablecloth.

He put his hand over hers, forcing it still, making her look at him. 'Darling, you've got a cookery book coming out in a few months that everyone seems to think will be a great success. You've had another commissioned, everybody is reading your column in the *Recorder*, and you've a fantastically handsome and successful fiancé. So what other failures are you worried about?'

She gave him a ghost of a smile. 'Three or four weeks ago I'd have said I was luckier that I would ever have believed possible. Now I feel it's all starting to disintegrate, that whatever touch I had has gone. I don't know where to go with this damn Finer Foods book. I haven't been able to help Joel Madoc over Marian Drax's death, I almost killed him with that meal the other night, and then I made a complete mess of my meeting with Jane Leslie this afternoon.'

William felt something go cold inside him.

'It seems to me,' he said slowly, 'that Joel Madoc is playing too important a part in all this.'

The startled look she gave him was not altogether reassuring. 'Not you as well? The last thing Jane said this afternoon was to keep my hands off Joel. What is it with everyone all of a sudden?'

'Could they perhaps see something you haven't realized?' William jerked it out, unable to keep his voice quite level.

'Oh, darling,' she turned the hand under his, dropping the knife and clutching at him. At the note in her voice, his world righted itself. 'I'll admit Joel Madoc is an attractive hunk of man but my heart is well and truly given to a tall policeman with dark hair, grey eyes flecked like a herring, and the kindest heart in the world.'

'Who loves you more than words can say.' For a moment he held her gaze with his, trying to pour all his emotions into his look, wishing he was some sort of poet. 'So what does anything else matter?' he suggested.

And at last he seemed to have got through to her. 'You're right,' she said softly, 'I'm such a fool. As long as I've got you what the hell does any of the rest of it matter?'

'Right! Now let's enjoy this evening.'

The duck arrived, it was tender and tasty, and they talked wedding plans for a little.

When he judged that Darina was more or less back to her normal, stable self, William said, 'Do you want to tell me a little more about that cutting you found this afternoon?'

For a moment he thought he'd blown it, that she was going to misjudge his motives. Then she gave a small, ironic smile. 'You can't kid me you think that will make me feel better, I know you too well. Could it really be important?'

'What do you think?' he asked steadily.

There was the briefest of pauses, then she said, 'It was an account of the trial of Jean Lovell for the murder of a man called Ken Bright. They had apparently been living together. She stabbed him with a knife she had been using to cut up ham for a salad she was making for the local delicatessen where she worked. The defence claimed Ken Bright had physically abused her over a period of many months, that she had needed hospital treatment on two occasions, once with third-degree burns from a boiling kettle he'd thrown at her, once with a nasty cut on her scalp after he'd hit her over the head with a broken milk bottle. According to the defence, on the evening he died, Ken Bright came back drunk and abusive, picked a fight and was coming at her with a bottle of whisky when she stabbed him.'

'Did the cutting mention any corroborative evidence for her story?'

'Neighbours testified they'd heard rows and said they'd seen Ken drunk on many occasions. The owners of the delicatessen told the court she had often turned up for work badly bruised and that over a period of time she had changed from an outgoing warm person into an introverted nervous wreck. They said they had tried to get her to see a doctor.'

'Any suggestions as to why she didn't just leave the man?'

'Apparently the house was hers and she was terrified that if she left she'd never get it back. The jury found her guilty of manslaughter with diminished responsibility and the judge gave her a suspended sentence of two years.'

'And you're sure the picture was of Jane Leslie?'

'If I wasn't before she caught me reading it, I certainly was afterwards.'

'She made a bad mistake there. Had she kept her cool and spun you a tale about keeping the cutting because people had mistaken the woman for her and she'd had some fellow feeling for the victim, you could well have swallowed it.'

'Yes, you just don't expect someone you know and like to turn out to have killed someone, even in self-defence.'

'Or she could have appealed to you, woman to woman, explained how she was trying to put her tragic past behind her and pleaded with you to keep her secret.'

'Her secret, yes!' Darina's eyes were suddenly alight. 'Do you think Marian Drax knew about her, that that was what she was referring to when she said that after she'd finished, Joel would never marry her?' William said nothing, just watched her mind turning over this idea, relieved to see his fiancée now appeared to be herself again. 'Marian could have gone to Jane and threatened to tell Joel the truth if she didn't break the engagement off. But if Jane was going to kill her, wouldn't she have done it then and there? Lost control as she did before?'

'Or was she afraid of incurring her suspended sentence and decided that this time she would be cleverer?'

'But how would she have set the trap? She would have to have got into the Finer Foods kitchen that morning.'

'Perhaps Jane told Joel everything.'

'Meaning he then decided to remove the threat to his fiancée?'

He nodded, watching the way she frowned slightly as she considered this idea. Then her nose wrinkled and she glanced at him from under her eyelashes. She seemed to come to some decision and looked him squarely in the face.

'I don't see Joel as murderer. Nor do I think there are two killers running round Finer Foods.'

William wondered if she was being deliberately obtuse. But there were pleasanter things to discuss this evening than this wretched case.

'We'd better have a chat with Melville tomorrow,' was all he said.

'We?'

'Of course, you are the one who found out about Jean Lovell.'

Chapter Twenty

The following afternoon, Saturday, William took Darina over to see Chief Inspector Melville.

The incident room had been set up in a village hall near Finer Foods.

The big man with watchful eyes welcomed them.

'Nice to meet you again, Pigram.' The two men had collaborated on a stolen-car ring a few years ago. 'Congratulations on your promotion, wouldn't have minded you on my team.' He led them to a quiet corner amongst the computers, the piles of paper, the people loading in reports and facts, the computers and boards stuck with photographs, room plans, lists, newspaper cuttings, and much else. 'I'm glad you rang, we were going to get in touch in any case to run through Wednesday evening with you. Can we take that first?'

Darina saw someone was getting ready to take notes of their meeting. She wondered why she had thought it was just going to be an informal chat amongst colleagues.

She and William gave all the details: the invitation Darina had issued, Joel's apparent ill health in the afternoon, how he had appeared that evening, what had been said, the time he had collapsed.

'I must say,' Melville commented at the end of the account, 'if he'd wanted to stage-manage the whole thing, it couldn't have come off better for him. You gave him all the wrong things to eat and he didn't hold back any of them.'

'Ah, you haven't experienced Darina's cooking,' William grinned.

'Then when he collapsed, he had two intelligent people on hand to do all the right things.'

'He didn't make sure we knew he was diabetic.' Darina could hardly believe what the Inspector seemed to be suggesting.

'No,' acknowledged Melville. 'That would have made the thing that much safer. But perhaps looked a bit suspicious?'

'And we could easily have left him to sleep it off. If I'd brought him a cup of tea in the morning and seen him still asleep, I might well have thought it a good idea to let him rest, not tried to wake him until much later. Which could have been too late?'

Melville nodded thoughtfully. 'There is that possibility, certainly. Could he have thought you maybe knew already he was a diabetic?'

'He said it wasn't a secret in the company, that they were used to seeing his insulin in his office fridge. But if you are thinking he staged his own collapse, what about the message that took Jane Leslie away?'

'What indeed?' queried Melville. 'When we first asked her, Miss Leslie refused to give us any details on where she went and why. That could either mean she suspects her fiancé of having sent the message or that they hatched the plot between them. But this morning she rang and said she would now be willing to give us the information. Two officers have gone round to take her statement.'

He stretched his arms above his head, wearily easing his shoulder muscles. 'This case may just be coming together. Ever since the start everything has pointed to Joel Madoc except for the fact that we could find no reasonable motive. The suggestion of an affair with Marian Drax seemed to offer interesting possibilities but it didn't really lead anywhere.'

'You mean there wasn't an affair?' asked William.

'I mean he admitted that they'd slept together once, at the height of his wife's illness. Said he'd turned to her for comfort and it had just seemed to happen. He said she'd understood and was no more in love with him than he was with her.'

'What made you believe him?' Darina asked carefully.

The Inspector considered her with a small smile. 'I can see you'll make a good policeman's wife, understand how we work. We had a chat with the Spanish au pair who works for Anna Drax Johnson. Her English is a bit what you might call idiosyncratic but she has no difficulty getting her point across. She quite obviously had an eye on Madoc herself but says she was warned off by Marian Drax. This was before his wife died. The girl said—' Melville reached for a thick pile of computer printouts and rapidly flicked through till he found what he wanted. ' "The aunt, she was such a copy of a woman, no blood that one. She thinks she keeps Joel all for herself. She try, when his wife die, I think she think he will marry her. But she is not enough woman for him, I could tell he have no interest. But he have no interest in me as well. I am perhaps too much woman for him." Latin temperament, I suppose.'

Darina could feel sorry for Marian Drax. She was younger than her sister, perhaps she had yearned after Joel for many years. Being made love to, even if for only one time, could have convinced her he felt the same.

'We haven't found anyone at Finer Foods who thought they were having an affair,' Melville was continuing. 'And if he was involved with her, someone would have noticed. The chemistry of these things is usually unmistakable and there's always the company gossip who picks it up. There were suggestions that she had a crush on him but that was thought only natural, he appears to exercise considerable attraction on most of the young women there.'

'He's a very attractive man,' Darina murmured.

'So it appears. Apparently his stepson-in-law's wife, Fiona Drax, described by one witness as a bit of a sex-pot, has taken to popping into the office at increasingly frequent intervals. The receptionist – what's her name, Maggie? – she says she went into Madoc's office one afternoon and thought she'd interrupted a most unbusinesslike session. However, Madoc claims she was the one pressing her attentions and they were nothing more than an embarrassment to him. According to him, he finally managed to send her away with a flea in her ear. We haven't talked with Mrs Drax yet, but if what he says is true it suggests he must feel strongly about this fiancée of his to be rejecting overtures from attractive females.'

'Strongly enough to kill to protect her reputation?' Darina was grateful for the touch of scepticism in William's voice and that he hadn't introduced the possibility of Joel deliberately inducing his own diabetic coma the previous evening.

The Inspector threw the computer sheets back on his desk. 'He has Italian blood,' he said as though that explained everything. 'There's one more interesting little fact in the light of what we now know,' he added. 'Jane Leslie popped into the office the morning Marian Drax was killed, said she needed some urgent supplies.'

134

'Did she go into the kitchen? She may have been on the premises but I didn't see her that morning.' Darina was getting a little tired of the way Melville appeared to be picking on stray details to bolster a theory she could only see as extraordinary.

'She said no, she only went to the warehouse to pick up the goods she wanted, and certainly we haven't found anyone who saw her near there.'

'What about fingerprints in the kitchen?' asked William.

'Only those you would expect from what we have been told. Members of the company, the cleaner, Miss Lisle here, and some from the agent from Hong Kong on the tap and cupboard door. He apparently turned off the water and tried to mop it up.'

Darina nodded. 'That was before I told him I thought we should leave everything as it was, after I noticed the burns on her hands.'

'I wish every member of the public would think ahead as quickly as you seem to do, it would make our job a lot easier.'

'But if Jane didn't go in the kitchen that morning, could she have had anything to do with the murder?'

'She was on the scene. It may mean absolutely nothing at all. On the other hand . . .' He made a small gesture with his palm that left the end of his sentence floating.

Two policemen came up to the desk, bringing with them a fresh whiff of the chilly October air.

'Ah,' said Melville expectantly. 'What is the tale from Miss Leslie?'

There was a quick glance at William and Darina before their attention was fastened on the Chief Inspector. 'She told us she had a message that a friend of hers in Suffolk was in trouble and needed her help. When she got there, the friend was fine and knew nothing about the message.'

'How had she received it?'

'A telephone call to the delicatessen, supposedly on behalf of the friend.'

'Male or female?'

'Couldn't say, the line was bad, but she thinks it was probably a man. No name was given. Miss Leslie said she was upset, didn't think to ask who was calling. She just set off immediately.'

'And the name and address of this friend that commands such instant obedience?'

The taller of the two policemen read out the details.

'Why the refusal to give us this information before?'

'First of all Leslie said she was scared, that she thought someone had been trying to get her out of the way so an attempt could be made to murder Madoc.'

The other policeman chipped in: 'But when we pointed out that this information could perhaps help us to track down a possible killer, she broke down and told us who the friend was. She said the real reason she hadn't before was because it meant everyone would now know she was actually Jean Lovell, not Jane Leslie.'

'So who was this mysterious friend?'

'The ex-wife of one Ken Bright.'

Darina sat staring at the officer. Ken Bright was the man Jane Leslie had been convicted of killing with a kitchen knife.

Chapter Twenty-One

According to Jane Leslie, Chief Inspector Melville was informed, Bright's ex-wife had contacted her after the killing and declared she deserved a medal. The two women had found common cause in their treatment at the dead man's hands and became friends. The only person Jean Lovell had retained from her old life when she changed her name was her lover's ex-wife and over the years the two women had exchanged regular visits.

The question was, who had known of the connection?

As far as Jane Leslie had been aware, no one.

Had Marian Drax known of her identity?

If she had, she hadn't said so to Jane. In fact, the delicatessen owner claimed, after their confrontation in the kitchen when the engagement had been announced, she hadn't spoken again to the Finer Foods' Financial Director. Yes, Joel Madoc knew her history, she had told him herself. And, yes, she admitted he had known about her friend. No, as far as she knew, Marian Drax hadn't broached the subject of her conviction to him either.

At the end of the report, Chief Inspector Melville had tapped his ball-point pen meditatively against his teeth. 'Do you consider she was telling the truth?' he asked the two detectives.

'I think so,' said the one.

'I'm not sure,' said the other.

'We'll have to have her in for further questioning,' decided Melville. 'And Madoc.'

'You still feel he could have staged his own collapse to avert suspicion he killed Marian Drax?' asked William.

'We shall, of course, look into the possibility somebody else could have doctored his insulin, but the case against him is building up,' Chief Inspector Melville said.

'Doesn't it seem very clumsy to kill someone in a way that points directly back to yourself?' Darina asked stiffly.

'Madoc appeared very soon after the body was found. It could be he intended to be first on the scene and remove the evidence before anybody else arrived or while they were being sent to call for help. One quick jerk could have removed wires and clips completely.' Darina couldn't help but remember how Joel had asked to be left alone with Marian's body.

'Surely, though,' said William, 'the burns on her hands would have told you she'd been electrocuted? In the absence of faulty equipment, you'd have been searching for some means that had been removed and be back with the same question, who had the opportunity?'

The Detective Inspector sighed. 'But would he have realized that? The man claimed to be something of an ignoramus where electricity is concerned. Obviously whoever fixed those wires knew exactly what they were doing but information on electrical circuits is easily available. He could have mugged up on the method and not realized we would be able to check none of the equipment was faulty. Then, when he finds that we are on to him, he stages this phony attempt on his life, trying to make it seem as if it was him the trap had been set for. That power failure came in very handy.'

'But aren't there several people with a motive for wanting to get rid of Joel Madoc?' Darina felt like banging the table to jolt him out of his one-track approach.

'Such as?'

'Anna Drax Johnson, for one. She was at odds with him over how the company was run and when Eleanor Drax died she must have expected she would be left her mother's shares. Peter Drax, her brother, was not at all happy with a drop in the company dividends, and now you say there are suggestions his wife was having an affair with Joel; money troubles plus sexual jealousy could be an explosive mix. And there's Michael Berkeley, he could also feel some right to the position of managing director, not to mention the possibility he could be embezzling funds and needing to prevent exposure.'

As she knew he would, the Inspector produced the awkward circumstance regarding all these suspects: 'Each has a cast-iron alibi for the morning in question. Drax Johnson and Berkeley left early for London and we've checked all their appointments, there's no doubt they were there. Dr Drax was holding his morning surgery, his arrival just before eight o'clock is attested to by

138

his partner and his head nurse.' Melville gave Darina an ironic look. 'You've forgotten to mention that Drax Johnson benefits from her aunt's estate, there's a house worth about £150,000 and a block of shares in Finer Foods; since the company isn't quoted, it's difficult to know what they are worth, what someone is prepared to pay for them, I reckon, but I'm willing to admit it could all provide a solid motive, *if* she needed the money and *if* she had the opportunity. So far we haven't been able to prove either. As for Berkeley, we are scrutinizing the accounts, but it's going to be a long job, our expert has never seen such a mess.'

'I thought cast-iron alibis were always suspicious,' Darina said.

'You've been reading too many detective stories. We have to take every alibi or non-alibi on its merits. In all these cases, the suspects were in the process of fulfilling a normal day's appointments. It's the out of the ordinary that particularly interests us.'

'So you think Joel Madoc killed Marian Drax to prevent her exposing Jane Leslie as Jean Lovell?'

'She was proving a nuisance in more ways than one.'

'But if he knew of her real identity, he obviously didn't care. Why should he have a motive?'

'Lovell obviously cared. Was prepared to go a long way to protect her new life.'

'What about some sort of timing device?' asked Darina in a last-ditch attempt to shake what was appearing a deep-seated conviction that Joel Madoc was guilty. 'Aren't there plugs that can be set hours ahead to turn on the current at a certain time?'

The Inspector looked at her patiently. 'Find me evidence one was used. There was no automatic timer in the kitchen when the SOCO boys went over it. The first people on the scene were the receptionist, who, according to your own statement, never entered the kitchen; the Far East agent, what was his name?' – he searched his memory for a moment before coming up with – 'Browne, that's it, and yourself. We've looked into both your backgrounds and, apart from the obvious business links, there's nothing to connect either of you with the deceased or any other member of the company. Browne has been agent for no more than a matter of months and his story that he flew in from Hong Kong that morning checked out.'

And, Darina reminded herself, he hadn't been in the kitchen alone anyway, no one had before the police arrived. The knowledge that she herself had been considered as a possible suspect came as a shock and it wasn't until later that she had to acknowledge the police had cast their net wide in their search for suspects. At the time it merely fuelled her slow-burning anger at their obtuseness.

'We are, of course, continuing to investigate other possibilities, particularly, as I said, regarding the insulin, but I have to tell you that it isn't looking good for Madoc. It's still all circumstantial but the case is building up.'

William was on his feet saying goodbye. Darina got up slowly, her rage igniting with the knowledge she was helpless in the face of officialdom. 'I suppose you realize,' she said with furious control, 'that if you are wrong, somewhere out there is a killer who could be planning a third attack on Joel Madoc?' She didn't trust herself to wait for an answer but marched out of the hall careless of whether her fiancé was following or not.

Outside she found William was close behind her. He unlocked the car and helped her into the passenger seat with a touch more than his usual care. There was silence as he started the engine.

'I'm not going to apologize,' Darina said mutinously as he drove back to the cottage.

'I wasn't going to ask you to,' he replied calmly.

'How,' she spluttered, 'how can he have such a closed mind?'

'He seems to be working on the available evidence,' he said carefully.

'He's not, he's ignoring half of it.'

'Are you sure you're not including as evidence your personal feelings regarding Joel Madoc and the other members of the firm?'

Darina opened her mouth to hurl more angry words, ask him if he didn't realize Joel's life was at stake, then closed it again. Was she just relying on gut instinct? Weren't the police patiently sifting through far more evidence than she could ever have to hand? What ammunition did she really have against the assumptions the Detective Chief Inspector seemed to be making?

'I just think that if you were in charge of the case, you would be looking more imaginatively at the evidence,' she said after a little. 'And don't give me that stuff about hunches only playing a part in crime novels.'

He flashed her a quick glance then said, 'Melville's approach strikes me as more than a little imaginative. His way of working isn't mine but it isn't my case.'

'You see,' she said triumphantly, 'you don't believe Joel is guilty either.'

140

'I said it isn't my case,' he repeated repressively.

'But isn't there any way we can help Joel?'

'Look, you heard Melville himself say they are looking at all the available angles. He may be personally convinced he has the murderer but he has to cover all the ground, check every possible—'

'Avenue, I know, I know,' Darina broke in. 'But if he doesn't think it's going to produce anything, it won't.'

'He's not a one-man band. You've got to trust the system.' William effected a clumsy gear change on his aged Bentley and added, 'Don't you think Melville mightn't be the only one with a one-track mind?'

Darina opened her mouth – then hastily swallowed what she had been about to say.

On the answering machine when they got back was a message from William's younger sister, Sarah. Could she come down the following day for lunch?

She arrived early on Sunday morning, fizzing with excitement.

'Ma's given me a trip to Hong Kong as an early Christmas present,' she announced. 'So I can visit Heather before I start this new job. I've been dying to go and they will be back home before I get leave from Brussels so this is my only chance. Ma says I deserve a treat. More likely she's hoping I'll meet some nice Army type who'll sweep me off my feet and convert me into a conformable little wife. As if I'd settle for that! Do you think I'm accepting her gift under false pretences?' She moved about the living room, laughing at herself, picking up and examining ornaments, books, and pictures, replacing them in slightly different arrangements.

Darina thought how restless she was, how different from William. But she liked her enthusiasm for life, her bubbling sense of humour and her refusal ever to accept the easy path. Brother and sister got on very well together and Darina was always happy to see Sarah.

'The thing is,' Sarah looked at her brother's fiancée, 'Ma wonders if you'd like to go with me. She's sent you a note.' She handed over an envelope.

Staggered beyond words, Darina opened and read the letter. It was generously worded. Joyce Pigram wanted to offer her soon-to-be-daughter-in-law an engagement present and would be so delighted if she would like to accompany Sarah to Hong Kong to meet Heather. It should be very enjoyable, particularly as William was so busy at the moment. Joyce Pigram ended by saying that Hong Kong would offer marvellous opportunities for buying linen and china at cheap prices and Heather would love to have her.

Wordlessly, Darina handed the letter to William, whose face lit up as he read it. 'There, I said she was delighted with you,' he said.

Darina turned to Sarah and raised a questioning eyebrow. 'I think Ma feels she put up the odd black last weekend,' the girl said bluntly. 'I wouldn't be surprised either if she thinks the example of nice Army marriages mightn't help you as well. Though she's an idiot if she does, Heather and Barry are hardly a typical service couple.'

'Do you like your brother-in-law?'

'Sure! He's really alive, I can just about understand why Heather puts up with having to move every couple of years and never being able to get on with a career of her own. You are coming, aren't you?'

'When are you going and how long for?' asked her brother as Darina seemed unable to respond.

'Some time next week. I thought for about ten days, it's hardly worth going for less but I can't afford more, I'm due in Brussels so soon. I'm booking my flight as soon as I know what Darina's plans are.' She looked pleadingly at her brother's fiancée, 'Do come, it'll be such fun.'

The prospect was dazzling. Hong Kong, a glimpse of the Far East, a chance to experience Oriental food; Darina had never been outside Europe, it was an incredibly generous invitation.

All Darina could think of was that there was a killer on the loose and that William wasn't going to accept that as a good reason for not going.

'I really can't leave this book, it's got a very tight schedule and even ten days is too long to be away.' It was no more than the truth. In fact the trip would effectively mean a two-week break in her schedule, what with organizing her departure, writing two of her cookery columns to cover the time she'd be away, then getting back into the swing of her work after she returned. She got up. 'I'd better ring your mother and thank her for her wonderful idea and say I'm only sorry I can't accept.'

'Don't do that!' Brother and sister spoke in unison.

Darina looked at them. William and Sarah exchanged glances. Darina drew a deep breath. 'You mean she'll take it as a rebuff?'

142

'I'm afraid she might,' said Sarah. 'You see, she'll find it very difficult to understand how writing a cookery book means you don't have the time to go.'

'I suppose she thinks either that it isn't important or that it's something you just toss off in the odd moment,' Darina said bitterly.

Neither William nor Sarah said anything.

Darina threw herself back into her chair and looked at them. She seemed to be in an impossible situation.

'Can't you really manage ten days?' William asked after the pause had lengthened dangerously. She didn't like the undercurrents she heard in his voice.

Was this what married life was going to be like? Just as William seemed to have learned how important her work was to her, was she going to have to make compromises because she couldn't teach his parents the same thing? And, if so, who was that being unfair to, him or her? And could she honestly say she was being totally open with him over her reasons for refusing to go?

'It'll be such fun,' Sarah said coaxingly. 'You'll like Heather and they'll give us a wonderful time. Think what you can get for your bottom drawer! And I'd like to have you with me,' she added slightly shyly.

'It does sound irresistible.' Darina made up her mind. 'I'll do it! What a rat I am not to have leapt at the opportunity as soon as you told me. It must have been the shock!'

One look at William's face convinced her she had made the right decision.

Having made up her mind, Darina went wholeheartedly ahead. She rang Joyce Pigram. The older woman's pleasure in her enthusiastic gratitude came clearly over the telephone. Then Sarah produced flight details and they got down to sorting out their arrangements.

Hong Kong was the only topic of conversation during lunch until the telephone rang half-way through and William was called away to deal with some crisis.

'I'm afraid it's always happening,' said Darina as she saw Sarah's disappointed face as William left without even waiting to eat the apple meringue she had made for pudding. 'It's just as well your mother didn't offer a ticket to him as well.'

'Ah, he's a man and not able to take off at a moment's notice,' said Sarah wryly. She and the tall blonde looked at each other in a moment of perfect communication. Darina knew they would enjoy each other's company on the trip. Would she get on as well with Heather, she wondered?

Once William's sister had left, however, she faced facts. Tomorrow she would have to call Joel Madoc and explain about going away. She could certainly justify the trip in terms of the book by virtue of the background information on Oriental food that Hong Kong would offer her. It was his vulnerability to attack from both the police and Marian Drax's murderer that worried her.

But she couldn't think of anything she could do that would help clear him, let alone expose the real killer.

The fact was, she was no detective.

Chapter Twenty-Two

On Monday morning, before she had had a chance to call Finer Foods' managing director, Charles Johnson had rung.

'Joel Madoc has put a hold on the book,' he said.

'Why?'

'He says that the company is in too much chaos at the moment to be able to think about major marketing promotions. I tried to explain that by the time the book is ready to launch on the unsuspecting world police investigations would be a thing of the past, but he wouldn't listen.'

As well he might not if he felt that the end of the police investigation could be his arrest for murder.

'Whatever happens, you'll get to keep the advance, of course. And don't junk any of your work, the project could well be resurrected in the future.'

Darina had put the phone down and sat looking at it. She supposed that the decision was not surprising. There was a sense of increasing unease at Finer Foods. Too many things were going wrong. Anna and Michael continued to work steadily, appearing unworried about faulty products, dissatisfied customers, decreasing cash flows. Were they welcoming the chance to show how in control they were in contrast to Joel's slipping command? For it was Joel who looked like losing his nerve and proving that he was unable to steer the company out of the trouble it seemed to be sinking into. There had even been reports of an uneasy meeting with dissatisfied employees, upset over not getting their dividend and worried about the future.

Under the circumstances, Darina had not been surprised when it appeared Joel had abandoned his usual abstemiousness and taken to alcohol the night of his collapse, particularly with Jane Leslie's calming influence removed.

Jane Leslie. Once the name had entered Darina's consciousness, it continued flickering there, like a dodgy fluorescent light.

She gave up trying to finish the article that had got to be completed before her departure for Hong Kong and thought again about the cancellation of the book. Had Joel used business uncertainty to get rid of her under pressure from Jane? At first she dismissed the idea. It didn't appear the sort of thing Joel would do. Oh, he might well dismiss her if he thought of her behaviour that afternoon in the same light Jane did. But he would say so, straight out, rather than using Charles Johnson as messenger.

Then she wondered if she really knew Joel Madoc as well as all that.

She picked up the telephone and rang him.

At the end of the conversation she was no wiser. He had been politely regretful over the decision, said he hoped that they would be able to go ahead with the book at a later stage, said there was no one they'd like better to write it. But a veil had come between them. Darina wished she had gone to see him instead of ringing. Without being able to see his face, she couldn't get through the courteous wall he was erecting. But she knew that in itself told her something.

Damn, she said as she once again put down the telephone. But at least she had been put in her place regarding the investigation. It was quite obvious Joel Madoc wasn't looking to her to solve the case. He even appeared unworried over possible further attempts on his life. She made a determined effort to clear her mind of everything but her article.

The next two days were frantically busy as she prepared for her trip. Then her mother insisted on having them over for supper to discuss wedding arrangements, refusing to leave it until Darina got back from Hong Kong. It would be too late, she said, making sure her daughter realized that to discuss the date with William's parents before her own mother had been thoughtless not to say slighting. Darina sighed and reflected that at least it meant she wouldn't have to cook a meal. She just hoped William wouldn't have to cancel. But he was with her as the pros and cons of London versus Somerset, small or large weddings, locations and caterers were chewed over.

By the time the Hon. Ann Lisle had filled several pages of a leather-backed notebook with her flamboyant writing, most of the main decisions had been taken. At last she laid down her pen, and took off the oversize glasses she wore for reading and laid them carefully on top of the notebook.

'I have some news for you.'

Something in her tone alerted Darina. She looked properly at her mother for the first time that evening.

Ann Lisle was a stylish woman, intensely concerned with her appearance, and determined to get the last ounce of satisfaction out of life. She had turned widowhood into a triumphal progress by filling her charming little house with friends, organizing charity functions with tireless efficiency, twisting the arms of any acquaintance to get what she wanted, and keeping at bay the depredations of the passing years with regular visits to beauty salons and health farms and the purchase of expensive clothes.

Now Darina looked beyond the style and saw that her mother was slightly flushed, that there was an unfamiliar softness about her. With a flash of understanding she knew what she was going to say before the words came.

Gerry, her mother's old friend, had asked her to marry him and they were going to have a small wedding in about a month's time.

Darina hugged her and said it was wonderful news. William was told to open the bottle of champagne that was waiting in the fridge and Ann Lisle made a quick telephone call to summon General Sir Gerald Stocks from his house round the corner. Retired from the Army for several years, living with his sister ever since his wife had died, he had been the widow's constant companion almost since he arrived in her village. It all couldn't be more suitable.

'Your mother wanted me here this evening,' he said to Darina, 'but I told her to get the business out of the way first and that she should tell you our news herself. What if you didn't approve, eh?'

She kissed him and said it was impossible not to approve and that it was going to be wonderful to have him to give her away at her wedding, then was touched by how he flushed with pleasure.

'Well,' William said as he drove them home a little later. 'Trust your mother to upstage your wedding!'

'Darling, it's great news, he's everything one could want, charming, reasonably well off, patient with all mother's little ways, and even manages to tease her occasionally. I thought they'd never get round to it.'

'So what are you being so quiet about?'

She put a hand on his thigh. William could always sense her moods, it made being with him very comforting and relaxing.

'I was just thinking about father. How he and mother were

147

always bickering, how unhappy he was by the end of his life at his failure to be all the things she wanted, at her disappointment at being married to a busy GP rather than a high-flying Harley Street consultant. He was such a lovely man and he needed someone quite different from her.'

'Now she's going to be happy and he's dead, is that it?'

'Something like that.'

William drove without saying anything for a little. Then he asked, 'Did he love her?'

'Desperately, even at the end. He was always trying to please her, planning little treats for her, buying her presents. And the awful thing is, I know he would want her to be happy now.'

'Then that's the way you must look at it.'

'I know, but somehow that doesn't make it easier.'

In the darkened plane thousands of metres above the earth, heading for what had been the USSR, Darina found herself wondering what Anna's thoughts had been when Eleanor married Joel. Had she felt not only that she had lost her lover but that her father had been supplanted as well? It could be a potent cocktail of emotion to carry around over the years. Years during which you saw your mother happy in a way she hadn't been in her first marriage to your father. Happy with the man you had wanted to marry yourself. And on top of all that, on her mother's death she had had to cope with Joel moving into the Drax company in the place she must have thought should have been hers.

Then Darina remembered Jane Leslie saying something to Joel about an unhappy first marriage. She couldn't have been referring to her relationship with Ken Bright, they had never been husband and wife. So that made two failed relationships for her. Darina knew nothing about the first but the second had sounded a nightmare. Now Jane was running her own business, very successfully, and had found a happy, stable relationship with Joel. To her it must seem the promised land, like green fields and water to the American pioneers after weeks traversing desert. Jane Leslie had killed in self-defence, what was she capable of doing to protect a happiness that must once have seemed for ever outside her grasp?

Marian or Joel, just who had that deadly electrical trap been set to kill?

And who had set it?

The sense of failure that had possessed Darina so strongly the previous week returned. It was ironic that only now, as it looked as though any chance to solve the crime had vanished, could she admit to herself how strongly the investigation had gripped her. And there was the Finer Foods book. Was that doomed to remain in its unsatisfactory state or would she have another chance to work it out?

And could Joel Madoc's life still be in any danger?

For a moment Darina wished she wasn't heading for the Orient.

The plane flew low over the Kowloon houses, so low Darina felt it could be going to land on top of them rather than at Kai Tak Airport. There were no high rises under this part of the flight path and she tried to imagine living with huge jets skimming over her roof day and night. So many people crammed so close together, what devastation there would be if a plane should crash. Then she gripped the arms of her seat a little more tightly as she saw how short the runway appeared before it ended in the glistening waters of Hong Kong harbour. She exchanged a quick grin with Sarah as the plane landed safely and at last allowed excitement to bubble through the stress of the journey.

There was nothing to stop both girls having the time of their lives. Darina didn't even have her work schedule to worry about.

Chapter Twenty-Three

Heather Thompson met them at the airport clutching the hands of two small boys.

Sarah rushed to greet her sister. The boys shrank shyly back as their aunt knelt to say hello, it had been nearly two years since they had last met. At five and six, that was a long time.

'How lovely to meet you at last.' Heather beamed at Darina, who couldn't help staring at her. 'I know,' her hostess said with mock despair, 'we think I'm a changeling.' She wasn't tall like the other Pigrams, or slim or dark. She was chubbily round with short legs and fair hair with a touch of ginger. But it curled in the way William's did when it needed a haircut and her grey eyes had the same dark flecks as his.

They had the luxury of a staff car to take them to the Thompsons' house in the New Territories. Impressions of fast roads, modern buildings, bustle and noise rushed past Darina as Heather tried to explain the difference between Hong Kong Island and Kowloon and how the New Territories weren't all that new but had been leased by the British in 1898, over fifty years after they had claimed the island, to provide much-needed space and amenities.

'I'll take you shopping,' Heather promised the girls, 'and we'll take the Star Ferry over to the Island, it's one of the sights of Hong Kong, much more fun than the tunnels.' She chattered away promising trips and parties and hopes for a sail on the Army junk.

Soon the car was driving through country with graceful trees, and low mountains on the near horizon. It was cosily craggy and untidily beautiful, not strange or threatening but definitely different.

The Thompsons lived in a largeish house set in a well-tended garden. There was a smiling Chinese housekeeper who produced English nursery food as though she had been born to it. 'It's what we all like best,' Heather apologized as shepherd's pie appeared for their first meal. 'I always have this when Sarah comes, it's my welcome food for her.'

'You'll have to get used to us,' Sarah said cheerfully, tucking into the dish with relish. 'As far as food is concerned, the Pigrams are philistines. You won't believe what she's done with William.' She turned to her brother-in-law. 'He's a gourmet these days, actually likes eating food with foreign names.'

'Pay no attention to her.' Heather offered second helpings of the shepherd's pie that were greedily accepted. 'She's a great tease.'

Darina thought what fun it must have been to grow up in a large family. The Brigadier asked her if she had any brothers and sisters. He was more sensitive than first appearances would suggest.

Barry Thompson was small and chunky like his wife and full of energy. He had a habit of whistling through his teeth as he moved about on the balls of his feet, as though poised for unexpected combat at any minute. He had played a boisterous game with his two sons the moment he came in, turning them into shouting, excited youngsters, all trace of their shyness banished. He had greeted Sarah with open enthusiasm and given every appearance of delight to meet Darina. 'Be good to have a fellow sufferer at the Pigram reunions, we can keep each other company.' The comment was light-hearted but Darina felt he had opened an unexpected door on the new life that awaited her as William's wife.

She could see she was going to enjoy being part of the large, noisy Pigram family but also that there would be times it could be overwhelming. There were family traditions, jokes and experiences she would never fully understand, a closeness between the siblings she could never share. It wouldn't matter because she liked them all so much, but it was something she had to come to terms with.

As she had promised, Heather took the two girls shopping. 'Hong Kong is just one huge market,' she said as they travelled in to the centre of Kowloon on the incredibly clean and modern underground that moved like silk between the stations, its doors opening exactly where markings on the platforms indicated they would.

'Hong Kong's been built on entrepreneurship, that's what

makes it tick. Their motto is they face the world, can sell to anywhere.' She took them through Kowloon's crowded streets, packed with smartly dressed Chinese and tourists from all over the world, past shops stocked with more consumer goods packed into one short stretch than the whole of Oxford Street could offer at sale time, past restaurants and fashion houses into an emporium that was a magic world of all the crafts for which China was renowned.

The girls pored over the fruits of poorly paid but highly skilled handiwork. Heather warned them not to buy until they'd seen other places then whisked them off to Barry's tailor so Sarah could arrange suits to power her way round Brussels in. Darina ordered silk shirts for William and herself.

Then it was off to the Star Ferry. The famous boat was small, shabby and basic. It took only minutes to cross the harbour, crowded with boats of all kinds, the waters flowing like a broad river between Kowloon and Hong Kong Island, interest on all sides. Crowning the island was the Peak, covered with greenery through which apartment blocks reared up and large houses could be glimpsed. The main commercial centre, crammed with sky-scrapers, clustered round the water's edge on the right of the island.

Darina and Sarah were led off the boat and into one of the tall towers they'd seen from the water. Inside, escalators winged them up from floor to floor through open atriums lined with smart shops, sparkling and gleaming with temptation. Heather introduced them to her favourite place to buy cloisonnerie, to the shop where Barry preferred to get his ties and belts, and to her jeweller. There Darina chose gold cuff-links as a wedding present for William and Sarah gave herself freshwater pearls the shape of plump rice grains.

Then they went out into the streets and the girls were shown small alleyways crowded with stalls selling bargains of all kinds. 'This is part of the fascination of Hong Kong,' Heather said. 'You get a glimpse of old China right beside the most modern of developments: tiny, narrow streets that are just a series of steps, crumbling buildings that seem to hold together by plaster and faith, shops so mysterious it's almost impossible to guess what they sell. Technology is underpinned with superstition, modern science lives side by side with ancient practices.'

It wasn't all shopping. The hurricane season was over, the heat of summer had lessened, and the air was fresh but still warm. There were days spent exploring the New Territories and sailing to other islands, social occasions meeting friends of Heather and Barry, and games with the two boys. Darina enjoyed playing with them, reading bedtime stories and answering innumerable questions about their detective uncle. She asked Heather if they couldn't be page boys at her wedding, they'd make a lovely group with the Johnson twins.

'I'm so sorry,' Heather said, 'I don't think we shall be able to come. The wedding's in February, isn't it? Well, we're leaving Hong Kong at the end of March and we couldn't fit in a trip home that near to coming back permanently, not even to see you and William get married.'

Darina stared at her. Nobody had mentioned anything of this. 'But we can so easily postpone everything until you get home,' she said. 'I can't understand why nobody suggested it. Your mother must have known!'

'It probably didn't cross her mind at the time,' Heather said comfortingly. 'Don't worry about it, I know William is anxious it should be as soon as possible.'

'But what's six weeks or so in a lifetime?' protested Darina. 'I would love you all to be there!'

'Why don't you give William a ring and discuss it?' suggested the Brigadier. 'I'm sure you'd like to talk to him anyway. Let's see, it should be about eleven thirty in the morning there, why not try his office?'

'I'd love to,' said Darina.

A moment later she was through and talking to her fiancé, who declared he'd been planning to ring her when he'd worked out what time it was her side of the world.

'It's all arranged,' said Darina after she put the phone down. 'He doesn't mind at all delaying the date if it means you can come.'

But she found it hard to concentrate on the conversation that followed. Her mind was concerned with the bombshell William had dropped at the end of their conversation. 'By the way,' he'd said, 'Joel Madoc has just been arrested for the murder of Marian Drax.'

153

Chapter Twenty-Four

Had the police uncovered more evidence, or had they finally decided what they had was enough?

At least if they were keeping Joel in jail he would be safe from any further attack.

But what would Jane Leslie be feeling? Her terrible past, a past she had tried to bury behind a new identity, was now uncovered, and the love of her life – Darina was convinced Joel was the love of her life – was under arrest. Her outcry against Darina when she found her reading that betraying cutting could only have been a rehearsal for her current emotions.

Somerset seemed a very long way away.

The rest of the evening unfolded pleasantly over a game of mah-jong, the Brigadier, as usual, winning. Darina found the clack of the ivory counters with their beautiful symbols counterpointing the shuffling of facts in the Finer Foods case around her mind. Suddenly an odd comment Jane had once made about her earlier life floated into focus and Darina realized she might have a source of further information about her right at hand.

'I met someone recently who said she had spent time in Hong Kong,' she said as the pieces were placed in their neat carrying case at the end of the game. 'I think her husband was in the Army, I wonder if you knew them? But then,' she added hastily, 'I suppose that's like Americans who always expect you to know their friend in England.'

'The Army's a very small place.' The Brigadier was pouring nightcaps for anyone who wanted them. 'And we all go round in concentric circles; chances are probably high we have met them, what's the name?'

'Jean Lovell.'

Barry Thompson looked at his wife.

'Oh, yes,' she said immediately. 'We knew Mike and Jean Lovell. Is she a friend of yours?'

Darina shook her head. 'I just met her recently. She seems to have had a somewhat unhappy life.'

'That's putting it mildly. Mike Lovell was, I'm afraid, not a nice man.'

'The Army doesn't often make mistakes over officers but we put up a real clanger there.'

'He seemed so charming when you first met him,' said Heather. 'He was all over me when I married Barry.'

'We were in the same regiment,' said her husband, bringing a whisky and soda over to his wife. 'I quite liked him at the start, it was only later one began to be suspicious. Then he married Jean and for a while things got better.'

'It was just after we came out here the first time, Barry and Mike were both majors and Jean and I spent a lot of time with each other, new Army wives together.'

'Did you like her?' asked Darina.

'We didn't have much in common. Food was Jean's thing, she loved going off to markets, trying new restaurants, and talking to the Chinese help about dishes and techniques. You know what I feel about all that so we weren't exactly bosom pals but, yes, I did like her, she had a very attractive warmth. Then our posting came to an end and Barry and Mike's paths parted. We met up again a couple of years later, in Germany. I was pregnant for the first time and found Jean was in the same condition. It made quite a bond. But she had changed, wasn't so open, and she seemed to have developed a remarkable propensity for falling over, or at least that's how she said she got the nasty bruises that kept appearing on her arms and face.' There was a brief pause then Heather continued, 'I think it was when she had her miscarriage we found out for sure that Mike was beating her up.' Darina heard herself give a small gasp.

'Ghastly, wasn't it?' agreed Heather. 'Several other things came to light at the same time. I won't go into details but Mike was chucked out of the Army. Jean had already started divorce proceedings. I kept in touch for a bit after she moved to south London. She bought herself a nice little house in Clapham with some capital she had inherited from her parents, I don't think she got much from Mike. The last I heard she was working in a delicatessen there. I had an ecstatic letter telling me she'd met a new man, loved what she was doing, and had never been happier in her life.' She looked at her husband. 'We were so pleased for her, weren't we, darling? That was while we were still in Germany and just as I was thinking I must get in touch when we got back to England, we got the news about the stabbing. It was a terrible shock.'

'We tried to help,' said the Brigadier, sitting on the arm of his wife's chair and drawing her against his side. 'There was damn little that could be done but we saw to it that she had a good lawyer and offered her help from regimental funds after it was all over. She refused, said she could manage and wanted to start again somewhere nobody knew her. We could understand that, of course. How did you run into her?'

Darina gave them a brief account of Jane Leslie, ending with Joel Madoc's arrest.

'Oh, the poor woman,' said Heather. 'Her talent for picking wrong men must amount to Olympic Games proportions.'

'I thought she'd got it right this time,' said Darina slowly.

The Brigadier looked at her sharply. 'You mean you think this chap is innocent?'

Darina nodded.

'So what are the police playing at?' asked Sarah excitedly. 'And what does William say?'

'It isn't his case, all he knows about it is what I've told him and he's picked up from the detective in charge.' She gave them further details, explaining just how black it looked for Joel. 'There doesn't seem any way anyone else could have electrified that sink but Joel.'

'You want some sort of self-destructing timer,' said Sarah.

'Like a piece of ice?' suggested the Brigadier, jumping up and going off to the drinks table. He took a chunk from the insulated bucket and placed it on the edge of the tray. 'Now, you'd need some form of insulation, of course, but if you could arrange that to hold apart two electrical connections, you could take yourself off and have established an unbreakable alibi by the time the ice melted, the insulation dropped away and the electricity connected. You probably wouldn't have long, though. What's the time lapse between the last opportunity for arranging the trap and when this woman died?'

The sheer ingenuity of the idea . . . Evidence that disappeared without a trace, like the frozen leg of lamb that was used for murder and then was roasting in the oven by the time the police investigation had started. Darina thought back to the various timetables she knew about. Suppose Joel had escaped the trap because of the power cut. That meant it could have been activated shortly after Joel started his session, after the secretaries had finished clearing up their breakfast; but it would have to have been set some time before the cleaner began her work, since she had still been in the kitchen when the secretaries arrived. Darina totted up times in her head.

'It would need about an hour and twenty minutes at least,' she said doubtfully.

They all looked across at the ice cube, already half melted on the tray.

'Would probably be much cooler over there, of course,' ruminated the Brigadier. 'And nothing to say you couldn't work with a much larger piece of ice.'

Darina thought of the size of the spring clips attached to the U-bends and shook her head. But the thought was still very appealing. 'It's definitely something to think about,' she said. 'I'll mention it to William, perhaps he could take it further.'

'Drax,' said the Brigadier meditatively. 'I ran into someone of that name in Hanover some years ago. He was in the medical corps.'

'That could be Peter, Joel's stepson,' said Darina. 'He's a doctor. I didn't know he'd been in the Army.'

'It was only a short service commission. He nearly got himself cashiered, though.'

'What on earth for?' A less likely candidate for courts martial than the quiet doctor Darina found hard to imagine.

'He had a most attractive little wife. There was some sort of an affair with a German and apparently Drax nearly killed him.'

'How?'

'He lit into the man. The wife got frightened and called the police. They arrived just in time to prevent the German having his head bashed in with a World War I shell case. If it hadn't been for the fact that the German wouldn't press charges, it could have been extremely nasty.'

'Why ever didn't he?' asked Sarah.

'Everyone felt it was slightly peculiar and there was a suggestion Drax had some information on him, something to do with illegal trade with East Germany. It was quite a talking point for a while.'

'Why did I never hear anything of it?' demanded Heather.

'It was before we were married, my angel, on my first German tour.'

'I had no idea life in the Army produced such marital discord,' said Sarah.

'Oh, it's not easy to be married to a soldier,' her sister asserted, with a sly look at her husband. 'But Barry is an angel,' she hastily added as he scooped up a handful of ice and advanced towards her.

At the weekend they went racing in a large party to the Sha Tin racecourse.

'What luxury,' declared Sarah, looking around the charming room situated above the emerald-green oval of the course and thronged with smartly dressed Orientals and Westerners sitting around tables of various sizes. Video screens offered perfect viewing of the races and bets could be placed in the room as well.

'It's all tote betting,' the Brigadier explained. 'Watch the combinations you're offered, there are all sorts of ways you can increase the possible pot by increasing the odds, which mostly means that all you increase is your losses.'

Along one side of the room was a buffet of monumental proportions. As Darina was examining the mainly Western-style food, she realized that the man standing beside her also studying the dishes was Patrick Browne, the Hong Kong agent for Finer Foods.

Chapter Twenty-Five

The agent looked straight at Darina and for a moment she thought he didn't remember her. But when you are nearly six foot tall in your stockinged feet and have long blonde hair few people forget meeting you, and after a few seconds his face brightened.

'Didn't we meet in rather distressing circumstances on my last trip to England?' he said. 'This is an extraordinary coincidence, what are you doing here?'

Darina explained, giving a wave of her hand towards the Brigadier's table. 'I've been having a wonderful time, but I'm delighted to run into you, I'm seriously lacking information on food. I've seen amazing shops selling all sorts of ingredients, including a vast variety of spices and dried and pickled foods, even snakes, and someone told me much of it is used as medicine rather than food but I'm afraid Heather and Barry can't tell me a thing, except that most of the food here is Cantonese and they find it very boring.'

'That's terrible.' He sounded quite shocked. 'Hong Kong has the greatest variety of Chinese cooking available anywhere in the world. And Cantonese chefs are the best in the world! I admit, though, that much of the cuisine here *is* Cantonese, that's because most of the Chinese in Hong Kong are from there, it's the nearest region. And it was the Cantonese who emigrated in the nineteenth century, to work on the railways in the Americas, dig out gold in Australia, New Zealand, and South Africa, or tin in Malaya. And wherever they went, they took their home cooking. Like us all, they prefer the food mother makes.'

'And they would have found Western food difficult to adjust to, it's so very different from Chinese,' said Darina.

Patrick Browne smiled. 'Indeed it is. But it has more variety than you would suppose from the average takeaway or even a high-class Cantonese restaurant. You could be in for a surprise when you start sampling food from other areas. All the regions have their own cuisine. Sichuan food, for instance, is very spicy. In Shanghai they go in for gentle and slow braising rather than rapid stir-frying and use a marvellous spicy wine. It's all to do with local produce and climate. Take, for instance, one of the most famous of Chinese dishes, Peking duck. In the area around Beijing a hot dry wind springs up in summer. Any duck you hang up around that time suffers instant dehydration, producing that wonderfully crispy skin when it's cooked. Westerners are advised to use a hair dryer to produce an effect that originally is quite natural.

'But though Chinese cuisine is rooted in local home cooking, it's very adaptable. You can eat the same dish in San Francisco, Sydney, and Southampton and it will be subtly different each time, reflecting local influences. All through her history, China has embraced new methods and ingredients: chilli peppers, saffron, aubergine, spinach, dill, sesame, garlic are just a few of the foreign influences that spring to mind.' He smiled at her self-deprecatingly. But he had no need to apologize to Darina about getting carried away by food.

'What about ingredients that always seem to sum up Chinese cooking, like the soy and black-bean sauces, for instance? Do these vary?' For Darina the meeting was like spring rain after a cold and arid winter, she hadn't realized quite how she had missed someone to talk food with. All contemplation of murder had receded to the furthermost areas of her mind.

Patrick Browne seemed only too willing to indulge her interest, he had the happy air of a man engaged in a favourite activity. 'Yes, indeed, there are various sauces, preserves, and pickles no Chinese cook can manage without. The home cook will still prepare most of them himself but there is a huge business producing commercial varieties for those who haven't the time or the skill to make their own. They are, as you say, essential. Chinese cuisine results from a careful balancing of yin and yang. You know about yin and yang?'

'It's the male and female, isn't it? Opposites?'

'Right, positive and negative, hard and soft, vigorous and yielding; most of Chinese life involves balancing these forces, including the preparation of food. So the same meal will use, for instance, ginger, which is yang, and spring onion, yin. Pickles will be used to balance fresh meat, sweet flavours will be balanced with sour,

160

plain with spicy. And in China the motto "You are what you eat" is taken to its most logical conclusion, which is why, as you said, you sometimes don't know if you are in a food shop or a pharmacy.'

'Where did your love of Chinese food come from?' Darina asked, by now as interested in a man who had such a patent enthusiasm for his subject as in his information. 'Was it being stationed in Hong Kong?'

'That helped, I suppose, but it really goes back to what I said about preferring the food of one's childhood. Mother loved all varieties of Chinese cuisine, she knew a great deal about it and was an inspired cook. Her repertoire was large and we ate food from other parts of the world as well but Oriental cooking was her favourite.'

'I once asked a Japanese woman I met in London what the difference was between Chinese and Japanese food,' said Darina, 'and she told me Japanese was "low food". I was trying to work out if that meant Chinese was "high" when I realized that, of course, she couldn't pronounce her r's!'

Patrick Browne grinned. 'I've never quite been able to get on with raw fish. Though really fresh – it has to be really fresh – sushi can be marvellous.'

'It must be a joy to work in an area that you enjoy so much,' commented Darina, then felt that was an echo of something she had heard in the not too distant past.

The ex-Army man's eyes gleamed. 'I was incredibly lucky,' he said. 'I couldn't have asked for anything better.'

Darina wondered if he had heard of Joel Madoc's arrest. It seemed he hadn't and was overwhelmed at the news. What a tragedy, he said, he'd been very taken with the glimpse he'd had of the Finer Foods chief. What would happen to the company now, he wondered?

Darina said it wasn't certain Joel would be convicted, the police could well have made a mistake.

'Really?' he asked her, startled. 'Not that I know much about it but I thought they were usually on pretty sure ground before arresting someone, particularly for murder.'

Darina was suddenly conscious they had been talking together for some time and that Sarah had developed a keen interest in who her companion was. She took Patrick over to their table and introduced him. It turned out he'd served with a couple of the other officers in their party and soon they were discussing Army postings, then the conversation became more general and Darina was amused to see Sarah drawing him out in a way that could only be called combatively flirtatious.

Oriental food was not her scene, she declared, there must be something else he was interested in.

Oh yes, one of the other officers declared slyly, there certainly was and no doubt Sarah would soon find out what.

The lawyer refused to be drawn on that and instead pressed Patrick to explain why he'd left the Army.

'Too limiting,' he said quickly, ignoring glances exchanged between others at the table. 'I felt I had talents, commercial abilities that were not being used.'

'Commercial abilities!' someone hooted. 'Come on, Browne, you were hardly able to organize wine for the mess! And your logistical skills couldn't move a body of men from Aldershot to Salisbury, Heaven knows how you get stem ginger from China to England!'

'Let's be fair,' said another judiciously. 'He's not entirely without talents. What about that competition he won in Germany?'

'Competition? What competition?'

'When we were overrun with all those mice?'

Patrick Browne held up a hand in mock surrender. 'Chaps, I think that's enough,' he said. 'Not fair to bore the ladies like this. In fact,' he turned to Darina and Sarah, 'I'm sorry but I should be getting back to my party.'

Darina asked if she could visit his office and have another chat about Chinese food and cooking, there were still many things she would like more information on.

He gave an apologetic smile and said he had to leave Hong Kong early the next morning and wouldn't be back for ten days or so. Would she still be visiting then?

'I'm sorry, as I said earlier, Sarah and I leave next Saturday.'

Patrick Browne promised to contact her when he was next in England and melted back to his party.

'The way that chap always lands on his feet!'

'What do you mean?' asked Sarah, her eyes on the agent's retreating back.

'I don't really want to tell tales.' The officer eyed her speculatively.

'But?' she pressed, giving him an amused smile.

He hesitated and someone else leant across the table. 'He

means Patrick's not safe with an attractive girl like you. His poor wife finally gave him the boot, landed him with alimony and school bills.'

'He may claim the Army wasn't using all his talents, but the fact of the matter is,' said the other officer, 'he was made redundant after the government service cutbacks. Bloody lucky to find that Far East Food Company job.'

'Yes,' agreed Barry Thompson. 'A lot of soldiers would be happy to find a well-paid position that would enable them to stay in Hong Kong.'

'Whereas many of the Chinese middle management have left,' Heather contributed from the other side of the table. 'Getting out in advance of 1997 when the Brits hand Hong Kong back to Beijing. The top people are staying and those low down in the scale haven't the opportunity to do anything else. It's the bright middle lot that are leaving. And leaving gaps that Europeans are filling. Patrick seems to have found one of them.'

'As I said, he always was a lucky dog,' reiterated the officer.

'And I'm sure it was he who won that competition,' insisted his companion.

'What competition?' The Brigadier sounded intrigued.

'The Great Mousetrap Contest when we were invaded by rodents. Someone declared we must be in Hamlin rather than Hanover and a magnum of the best burgundy was put up for the gadget that killed the most mice.'

' "Build a better mousetrap, write a better book, preach a better sermon, and though you live in the depths of the forest, the world will beat a path to your door," ' quoted Heather. 'And just what did Patrick devise?'

'He proved his brain can work when he wants it to because it was a miracle of neat thinking. Two metal plates were fixed either side of a block of wood, with the bottom plate, the base of the trap, much larger than the top. A negative wire was attached to that and a positive one to the top, which had a nice piece of cheese fixed to it. The whole arrangement was set like an island on a tray of water, and the trap set by the wires being plugged into a socket. Among comes Mr Mouse, whiskers all a-quiver, and sees the cheese. Seems quite simple to have a nibble, all he has to do is pad through the water, stand on the bottom plate, raise himself up, put his wet front paws on the top plate and reach for the cheese.'

'Except,' said his fellow officer, unable to resist taking over the story, 'by then he had completed the circuit and electrocuted himself. He got thrown off the plate by the shock and the trap was all ready for the next unwary rodent. By the time morning came the floor was littered with dead mice and the trap had finally shorted out with a particularly big mouse who was found stiff and dead caught between the two lethal plates.'

Darina's mouth felt dry. The principle of the trap was identical to the one set up with the sinks in the kitchen at Finer Foods. But Patrick Browne couldn't have had anything to do with Marian Drax's death, he had only flown in from Hong Kong that morning. She remembered Chief Inspector Melville saying that they'd checked he actually had been on the plane and that they hadn't found any personal connection between him and Finer Foods. She looked across the room, to the table the agent had indicated belonged to his party. There was an empty place and Patrick Browne was nowhere to be seen.

Chapter Twenty-Six

Patrick Browne did not reappear that afternoon. Darina followed the racing, bet on horses, lost her money, recouped it with a dramatic win on the last race following a tip the Brigadier said he'd had from a good source, and chatted as sensibly as she could with only half her attention.

The following day, Monday, Darina felt it would be a good idea to give Heather and Sarah some time together, the sisters must want to be on their own for at least a little while. And there were several things she wanted to do that were unlikely to interest Sarah.

So Darina took the underground train into Hong Kong Island on her own. The Museum of Tea Ware offered a comprehensive collection of teapots and cups illustrating the development of tea drinking in China. As she made notes for a possible article, Darina's mind turned over the ideas she had been working on for the suspended Finer Foods book. Patrick Browne had started her thinking about the development of Chinese cuisine, the way it had absorbed ingredients and ideas from abroad, had exported its style all over the world and then adapted to new local ingredients and conditions. All around her, in this civilized little museum, she could see similar elements at work.

Her mind in a ferment of new ideas, Darina wandered out of the museum, pausing for a moment to appreciate how the gracious colonial house, its verandas built to provide maximum protection from the devastating heat and humidity of summer, now had as backdrop the skyscrapers of modern Hong Kong, their indoor temperatures automatically regulated throughout the year.

She made her way into the recently built park that swept down the lower slopes of the Peak and encompassed Flagstaff House, found a convenient seat, and admired the variety of landscaping while once again considering the various events surrounding

Marian Drax's death and Joel's recent collapse. Until they were sorted out, there would be no chance of resuming work on a book that had at last taken fire in her imagination.

As she listened to the bird song from the immense aviary – wings of netting over walkways latticed in the Chinese style – and rehearsed the facts she knew, considered the personalities involved, a new idea surfaced; and she realized that Hong Kong might have opened her eyes in more ways than one.

She went back to the Museum of Tea Ware and asked in the souvenir shop if they had a Hong Kong telephone directory. A smiling assistant produced what she said was the latest edition.

Darina leafed through the pages looking for Far East Foods, then found there were two companies with almost identical names. There was Far East Foods and there was also The Far East Food Company, one above the other in the book. Which was Patrick's firm? She looked at the addresses. She recognized the name of the building housing The Far East Food Company as one in the Central area, where Heather had taken them to her jeweller; it was only a short distance from the Museum. The other address meant nothing to her. She asked the helpful assistant if she could tell her where it was.

The girl made a little expression of distaste, it was not a nice area, she said, and quite a little way away. She seemed to think Darina would have no interest in going there and made no effort to give any directions.

Darina made a note of both addresses and telephone numbers and decided to pay a visit to the company in the nearby building.

The directory of offices displayed on the ground floor told her which floor and corner of the building she could find The Far East Food Company and eventually a buzzer let her into a smart reception area with a young Oriental girl working behind a desk. She looked up as Darina entered. 'How can I help?' she asked.

Darina had given some thought to her approach and had decided to enquire if the company was the agent for Finer Foods. If it was, she would explain that she was writing a book on their products, was in Hong Kong on a short holiday, and had thought it might be an idea to see if anyone there could help her with some information on Finer Foods' Oriental lines. Should Patrick Browne, after all, be in Hong Kong, it would be interesting to see what story he produced after telling her he had to leave the city.

166

But Patrick Browne's name was not mentioned. Darina was asked to wait a few moments and then a middle-aged Chinese, dressed in a beautifully cut suit, his smooth face courteously concerned, came into the reception area and asked what he could do to assist her. Darina repeated her story.

'Ah, I would be very pleased to be of any help I can,' he said. 'My name is Mr Wu and I am a director of this company. Please, come this way.' He took her to an office in the corner of the building with a staggering view of the harbour. Darina gasped at the sight, walked straight over to the window, and stood looking across the harbour to the bustle of Kowloon, at the airport with its constant stream of planes taking off and landing, then at the water with its myriad of craft.

'How do you get any work done, with such a view?' she asked.

Mr Wu smiled, his bland face creasing into engaging wrinkles, his eyes alive with intelligence. 'After a number of years it is almost possible to work without noticing it. But not quite.'

He offered her a seat.

'I think I know one of your executives, Patrick Browne, but I believe he is out of town,' Darina said, deciding not to get bogged down in details of food before attempting to broach the main object of her visit.

'Mr Browne? You know him? But he does not work for us!'

'He doesn't?'

'No, Mr Browne has his own company. He is Finer Foods' representative in Hong Kong.'

'But, forgive me, Mr Wu, your receptionist said you were the Finer Foods agents here.'

He sat down behind a large modern desk, placed his arms in front of him with hands clasped, and looked benignly at her. 'That is so.'

Darina decided to approach the subject from a different angle. 'Would it be impertinent of me to ask you to explain the difference between a representative and an agent?'

'You have not talked with Anna Drax Johnson on this matter?'

'The subject has never come up.'

'And you say you are working with Joel Madoc, the new managing director?' Mr Wu also appeared not to have heard of his arrest.

'He was the one who commissioned the book I am working on.'

'Ah!' Mr Wu looked down at his clasped hands, opened the

167

palms and left the fingers laced together. He appeared to be considering the best way to explain matters. 'Perhaps I will tell you what has happened, then you can judge the difference for yourself.'

It appeared that The Far East Foods Company had been agents for Finer Foods for many years. 'We negotiate with suppliers, check quality, research alternative sources, find new products, arrange delivery, shipping, payment, everything. Eleanor Drax has visited us several times. We have arranged for her to see many suppliers, visit growers of ginger, manufacturers of soy sauce, and other facilities. She appeared to be very happy with the service we provide and we had, I think, a very satisfactory relationship. It was a great tragedy she died so young.'

Mr Wu got up from his desk and walked over to his stunning view. He looked at boats moving in the harbour. Darina waited. After a few minutes, he turned to look at her again. 'Shortly after her death, her daughter, Anna Drax Johnson, visits me here and explains that the company is undergoing reorganization. That her stepfather, Joel Madoc, is taking over as managing director and they have decided to have their own representative here, Major Browne. She assures me it will make no difference to our business with them, except that everything will in future go through Major Browne. And it is Major Browne who will liaise with them in England.' He looked out across the bay again. 'It seemed a little strange to us, expensive for them to employ another link in the chain and odd that Major Browne's company should bear a name so similar to ours, but Miss Drax Johnson seemed very happy with the arrangement. And put beside the total annual business our company does with Finer Foods, the salary of even a highly paid executive is not considerable.'

Darina was thinking swiftly. 'Do you mean, Mr Wu, that you invoice Major Browne's company for all the goods you sell Finer Foods and he pays for them?'

A certain respect came into Mr Wu's face. 'Exactly, Miss Lisle.' In the one short phrase he managed to indicate that he found it difficult to comment further but there was a great deal more he wished he could say.

'Have you discussed this arrangement with Joel Madoc?'

Mr Wu came back to his desk and sat down again. 'After Miss Drax Johnson left I rang the company. Mr Madoc was abroad on business but I spoke to Marian Drax, the Financial Director, and asked if we could have some official confirmation of the arrangement. Not that we doubted in any way Miss Drax Johnson's authority, she is Marketing Director, after all, but we like to be orderly in these matters. She assured me such a confirmation would be sent immediately and so it was. I also wrote to Mr Madoc and invited him here, saying we should be so delighted to meet him and perhaps arrange for him a visit to China, as we had done for Mrs Drax. I received a charming letter saying he hoped to visit us when he had managed to settle down in his new position.' Mr Wu clasped his hands on the desk in front of him again. 'I have not heard from Mr Madoc since. And now all our contact is solely with Major Browne.' Mr Wu looked straight at Darina.

'Maybe these matters are no concern of yours but this is the first opportunity I have had to speak with what could perhaps be called an unofficial representative of Mr Madoc.'

'I have been, am, working very closely with Joel Madoc,' Darina assured him, glad she was wearing a linen suit rather than one of the more casual dresses she had brought with her. 'Is there something in particular worrying you?'

'A few weeks ago I heard via one of our agents in the field – you must understand that after so many years in the business we know everybody and have contacts everywhere – that Major Browne was now buying certain products direct, not through us, and that the quality of these products was highly questionable. This worries me and so I rang Miss Drax Johnson. I thought perhaps she might not be aware of Major Browne's actions.'

'And was she?' prompted Darina as Mr Wu hesitated again.

'It was difficult to say. She assured me she was grateful for my call but that there was nothing for me to worry about and also hinted, no more than that, that the arrangement with Major Browne would not be continued for very much longer.'

'You didn't talk to Joel Madoc himself?'

'Since her mother's death, Miss Drax Johnson has been my contact with the firm.'

It was just like the Army or the police, Darina decided, lines of demarcation decided the way actions were taken.

Mr Wu leaned forward over his desk. 'I have given you these details, Miss Lisle, because I am concerned. I am concerned for the good relationship of this company with Finer Foods. I am in something of a quandary and do not know the situation in the company in England. Major Browne, of course, will tell me nothing. But you can see that I am not in a happy position. I have been very frank with you and I would be delighted if you could be equally frank with me.'

What he was asking for, of course, was assurance that Anna was not double-crossing Joel, that if he approached the Managing Director with the full story of what was going on in Hong Kong, he wouldn't find immediately afterwards there had been a boardroom revolution and that Anna was now heading the company. On the other hand, he didn't want a triumphant Joel Madoc to discover that Mr Wu and his company had been conniving in some way with Anna to defraud Finer Foods of profits. Either way he could find that he had lost the Finer Foods business.

Just where did Anna Drax Johnson stand in all this? And what exactly lay behind the appointment of Patrick Browne?

Chapter Twenty-Seven

After rapid thought, Darina decided that her only option with Mr Wu was to be economical with the truth.

'Finer Foods are in something of a state at the moment,' she said. 'There has been a terrible tragedy. I'm sorry no one has told you.' She gave him brief details of Marian Drax's death. 'The police are investigating and hopefully the matter will soon be resolved.'

Mr Wu fixed his eyes on her and she could see he was trying to assess the implications of the situation for him and his firm.

'But as soon as there is an opportunity, I will have a word with Joel Madoc,' Darina promised. Mr Wu's face was inscrutable but she knew he and she understood each other.

Sitting on the underground going back to the Thompsons' house Darina had much to think about. Without him mentioning the matter, she knew Mr Wu considered she was now his emissary to Joel Madoc. Whatever happened at Finer Foods, he felt he had guarded his position.

The arrangement Mr Wu had described could easily account for Finer Foods' declining profits, or at the very least go a considerable way to explaining them. The Far East Food Company's invoices to Patrick Browne's so conveniently named organization had only to be reinvoiced at a higher price to Finer Foods. The accounts department there would notice the slight difference in name and the different address but Darina doubted that anybody else would, or would think twice about it if they did. Price rises could easily be blamed on conditions in China. As long as Marian's authority was unchallenged, the invoices would be paid; Patrick Browne would pay Mr Wu and, presumably, himself. Then, what happened to the difference? Mr Wu had suggested there were large sums involved, what was left over after the expenses of the operation had been paid could be considerable. Who was pocketing that money?

Darina considered what she had been told. Anna had informed Mr Wu about the change of procedure. Marian Drax had provided confirmation of this arrangement. Mr Wu had spoken with her on the telephone, he had said, that meant it wasn't a case of somebody forging a signature on a letter, Marian really had been involved. And the setting up of the arrangement had been timed for a period when Joel Madoc was away from the office so Mr Wu would be unable to speak to him.

Had Anna and Marian set up the scheme to defraud Finer Foods? They were major shareholders so in a way they would be defrauding themselves, particularly if the company had been placed in jeopardy. Had they done it alone or with other directors such as Michael Berkeley? He seemed to have a certain amount of contact with Hong Kong; could he have been fooled by the new arrangements or was he part of them?

Peter Drax might also be in on it. Had it been planned for personal gain or as a way to evade tax? But Darina had no idea what the tax arrangements were in Hong Kong and maybe the plan had nothing to do with siphoning off profits. Maybe it had been conceived as part of a move to oust Joel, to make it look as though the company was losing money under his directorship. Anna's hint, if Mr Wu had understood her correctly, that the arrangement might not last for much longer, could support this theory. There was certainly no doubt but that Joel had appeared to be losing control of the situation, even before he was arrested.

The fact that Patrick Browne was saddling Finer Foods with inferior products (no doubt including the odd-tasting soy sauce and the consignment of goods Joel had been worried about the night he had collapsed) could mean that he was taking the opportunity to develop additional business on his own behalf. On the other hand, it could all be part of the plot to prove Joel Madoc was unable to run the company.

At this point Darina began to wonder if what she had uncovered threw any light at all on the mystery surrounding Marian Drax's death or merely provided further complications.

Had Anna set the trap to remove the other person who knew what was going on? Perhaps also to inherit her aunt's shares and estate? If so, Marian had been the intended victim all along.

In that case, what part did the substitution of Joel's insulin with water play?

Could it be that, having got rid of Marian Drax, Anna realized proper accounting methods could uncover the Hong Kong situation and so had decided to remove Joel from the scene as well, thus preventing exposure and giving herself total control? There could be a certain logic to this if you ignored the fact that Anna had been in London on the morning of Marian's murder.

What if Peter Drax or Michael Berkeley had also been involved in the scheme? Could they have conspired with Anna in murder as well as fraud? Or had one of them had his own reasons for removing the accountant and Joel? Michael Berkeley had seemed genuinely devastated by Marian's death, though, and there was no ignoring the cast-iron alibis that both of them, like Anna, had been able to produce for the morning Marian Drax had died.

And exactly what was Patrick Browne's role in this matter? Could he merely be an innocent bystander who just happened to be in the right place at the right time when the position of new agent came up?

Darina was convinced it hadn't happened like that, everything had been far too neatly arranged. Mr Wu had said Anna's visit to Hong Kong had been shortly after Eleanor Drax's death. Everything was already in place then and therefore must have been organized very quickly. That suggested somebody in the plot must have known about Patrick Browne's availability.

Darina considered what she knew about the ex-Army man. A womanizer with more than a touch of recklessness who, it was claimed, had invented a clever mousetrap that was almost a prototype for the way Marian Drax had been killed.

And who had been on hand when her death was discovered.

For one devastating moment it was as though the air had been sucked from around Darina, leaving her beached like a fish, unable to breathe. Cold shivers travelled along her spine and left her trembling; had she not already been sitting down, she must have fallen. It was horribly clear to her now how Marian's death had been arranged. How could she have been so stupid?

Her blindness could have placed Joel's life in danger for a second time and perhaps it was only due to his arrest that he had been saved from yet another attempt.

Then Darina forced herself to think again. She must be particularly careful now, there mustn't be another mistake. Could she have things wrong, could Marian Drax have been the intended victim all along? After all, it seemed certain she had been involved in a clever scam and one crime often led to another.

Chapter Twenty-Eight

Somehow Darina managed to get herself back to the Thompsons' house, her sense of failure crushing any feeling of enjoyment in her day, her mind wrestling with the problem of what to do now.

Heather saw immediately that something was badly wrong, told her to sit down, and instructed Sarah to get a large whisky. 'What's happened? You haven't had an accident have you?' She took the glass Sarah had brought and pressed it into Darina's hand. 'Now don't say anything until you've had some of that.'

'It's nothing,' Darina protested, trying to pull herself together. 'I'm fine, really, it's just that I've had a bit of a shock. Could I ring William, Heather? I'm sorry to ask but there's something I've got to tell him.'

Heather was only too happy there appeared to be something concrete that might help her guest recover from her present state.

Darina rang William's office, praying he would be there, forcing her mind to become cool and logical, knowing she couldn't afford incoherence. The relief of hearing her fiancé's voice threatened to unsettle her. But by briefly concentrating her mind on a particularly lovely tea pot in white porcelain with a lion on its lid that she had seen that day, she managed to keep her calm and finally produced her story with all the control of a demonstration chef.

'So you can see,' she said finally, 'how this could throw a completely different light on things.'

'But there's no evidence to support what you suggest,' said William. Only the concern in his voice stopped Darina from screaming down the telephone.

'But doesn't it make sense?'

'So does the case the police have put together against Madoc.' But William must have felt Darina's distress humming along the telephone wires, for he added, 'Look, I'll ring Melville later and tell him exactly what you've said. There are definitely angles that he will want to investigate. You're back at the weekend, aren't you?'

'Yes, on Saturday, unless you think I should fly back immediately?'

'No, under no circumstances. See if you can find out anything more about this fellow Browne before you get back, Barry ought to be able to help there, you'd better tell him what it's all about. You can trust Heather to keep her mouth shut when it matters as well. And, darling?'

'Yes?'

'Don't worry about this, you really have nothing to blame yourself for.'

Easy for him to say that. A moment later Darina severed the connection, William's disembodied voice still vibrating in her ears.

She got up from Barry Thompson's desk and went into the living room, to find the Brigadier was now home and as anxious about her as the others. She unconsciously straightened her shoulders and launched into the full story.

By the time Sarah and she flew back to England at the end of the week, Darina had come to terms with what she still looked on as her incredible stupidity. It was in the past and what mattered was what happened now.

With her she had a folder of notes the Brigadier had collated on Patrick Browne. Not that they seemed to amount to more than she had already learned but there were details on his progress through the Army, some mundane facts such as his next of kin and a few quite flattering remarks on various aspects of his career.

Darina said goodbye to Sarah at the airport with real affection. She had enjoyed getting to know both William's sisters and was going to be able to thank her future mother-in-law with genuine fervour for her unexpected gift.

William met her off the train, his eyes widening as he took in her extra luggage. 'Wait till you see what's coming by sea,' Darina said after she'd kissed him. 'I've bought some wonderful china and linen and all sorts of other things.'

'Have you had a good time?'

'Marvellous, the Thompsons couldn't have been kinder.'

She managed to wait until they'd got home before asking what the situation was with the Marian Drax case.

'Melville isn't very pleased with you,' said William lightly as he got them both glasses of wine.

'That's only to be expected. But what is happening?'

'There's been overtime put in on Finer Foods' Hong Kong accounts. They think now that the new arrangement is creaming off a sizeable chunk of revenue. Melville's in touch with the Hong Kong police to see what can be found out about the financial arrangements at that end, who are the company shareholders, what's happening to the profits, etc.'

'Has he approached Anna?'

'Not yet. I think he wants more information at his fingertips before he confronts her.'

'What about Joel?'

'Still under arrest.'

'What!'

'The Hong Kong information may prove just a red herring as far as the murder is concerned.'

'But surely, what I told you about Patrick Browne must be true.'

'You have no evidence.'

'What evidence do they have against Joel? I should have thought they could prove just as tight a circumstantial case the other way.'

'There's the little matter of who set the trap,' pointed out William. 'There is no doubt that Patrick Browne was flying from Hong Kong when those wires were arranged.'

Darina forced her tired mind to concentrate on the possibilities. 'The difficulty is I still can't work out who is behind it all. There is, I admit, a remote chance the intention was to kill Marian but it seems much more likely that it was all set up for Joel, that the insulin switch was another attempt, else why was Jane deliberately lured away?'

'We only have her word that she was.'

Darina stared at him then sighed, 'Oh, it's no use, I'm too tired tonight. Let's discuss this in the morning.'

'I've got a meal ready for us,' William said, rising on his long legs. 'At least, it will be ready in a few minutes.'

He led the way into the kitchen, where the table was already laid, with two late roses in a glass vase for graceful decoration. Salad was in a bowl and a large chunk of best Cheddar cheese waited with biscuits. By the stove were two chicken breasts together with mushrooms and cream. Darina watched in amazement as he lit the stove, sautéed the mushrooms, then the breasts of chicken, dressed the salad while the chicken was cooking, added some cream and seasoning to the meat and mushrooms, served the result on two plates, garnished them with fresh parsley, placed them on the table and waved Darina to sit down.

'Wine for madame? A little fresh bread? Anything else madame would like?'

'Madame can't think of a thing. Madame is just overcome with how wonderful everything is and very, very glad to be back.' She took a big mouthful of the food, then said, 'This is really good, darling. Your sisters would be amazed. Do you know Sarah told Heather you'd become a gourmet?'

'I can imagine only too well, the trouble is they're still on nursery food. I don't think they'll ever change, it's what we were all brought up on and they and Dad still like best.'

'Early conditioning makes all the difference; if one's mother is really interested in food and cooks all sorts of different and exciting dishes, it can give the children a taste for cooking and other people's cuisines that lasts all through their lives. I remember—' Darina stopped in mid-sentence, her fork poised in the air, a look of excited comprehension on her face.

'William, darling, I think I've got another piece of the puzzle!'

Chapter Twenty-Nine

Through the Delicatessen's door Darina could see Jane Leslie serving at the back of her shop. It was late Monday morning and there were few customers. Darina had timed her visit carefully.

She walked up the shop to the counter where Jane was returning a large joint of roast beef to the chilled cabinet and stood quietly until the customer had been served. Then Jane looked up and saw her.

Darina was shocked at the change in the woman. All the plump prettiness was gone. This was someone on the shores of despair with haunted eyes and wrecked face.

Jane said nothing, just stood waiting as though nemesis had arrived and must now be served with whatever bitter goods were demanded.

'Can we talk privately for a few minutes?' asked Darina.

Jane told one of her assistants she would be upstairs and led the way to her flat. She gave no greeting, asked for no explanations, merely sat in a chair and waited.

Darina sat also and without emotion gave a short account of her visit to Mr Wu and the realization that had come on the underground train back to the New Territories. At the mention of Heather Thompson, Jane raised her hopeless eyes and for a moment Darina thought she would say something. She paused in her account but Jane's gaze slipped back to contemplating the empty fire grate and after a little Darina continued with her story.

When she had finished, she waited for Jane to react. There was silence.

At length Darina said, 'Do you understand what it means?'

'I understand what you think it means.' Her tone was flat, contained no spark of hope.

'Someone had to have known of your past, not just who you were but also your relationship with Betty Bright. If only we can identify who that was, we shall have the murderer and Joel will be free.' Still there was no response.

'You can be together again.' Darina tried to get through the despair to the traumatized woman beneath.

Another little silence.

'All I'm interested in,' Darina persisted, 'is the truth, in discovering who killed Marian Drax and why.'

'Yet you wouldn't help Joel when he asked.'

At last, thought Darina with relief, a sign that there was still a woman inside this shell. Jane's voice was scornful and she looked directly at her visitor.

'I didn't think I could. And look how right I was, at what a mess I've made of everything.'

'So why have you come here?'

'Because I want your help.'

'My help! I've never been any help to anyone. Every relationship I've ever had has ended in disaster.'

'I know life has been very unkind to you,' Darina said gently. 'Heather told me about your first marriage, what you suffered, how you lost your baby and everything.'

As though she had pressed a button, huge tears began to run down Jane's face. She made no attempt to hide or brush them away and at first they were silent. Then sobs began to break through. She wrapped her arms around herself and rocked slowly back and forth. Long, shuddering howls of pain and anguish that seemed to have been bottled up for years were painfully released.

Darina let her cry. She came and sat on the arm of Jane's chair and held her, making soothing noises, hoping that some comfort would seep through.

When the intensity of the woman's grief began to lessen, Darina went and found her kitchen and made some tea.

When she returned to the living room, Jane was lying back in her chair in an attitude of complete exhaustion, her eyes red and puffy, her face swollen.

'Have you had anyone to talk to since Joel was arrested?' Darina held a cup of tea towards her.

Jane managed to sit up in the chair and take it. She shook her head. 'He was released on bail two days ago but I haven't seen him.'

'Why not?'

'All I bring him is disaster. If it hadn't been for me, he wouldn't be in this mess now.'

'What happened had nothing to do with you. The murderer used his knowledge of your past, that's true, but if you hadn't been on the scene, some other tool would have been found.'

Jane said nothing.

'Joel knew about your past, didn't he?'

The woman nodded. 'As soon as he seemed to be serious, I told him. I had to.'

'And did it make any difference to his feelings?'

'He said it didn't, said it was like his diabetes, a fact we could live with, but ever since Marian died I've felt it between us.'

'That was probably your imagination.'

'Maybe.' Jane didn't seem interested enough to argue the point. 'So, what is it you want from me?'

Darina could see an effort being made to pull herself together again. Whatever else, Jane was a survivor.

'I want you to come with me to visit your friend, Betty Bright.'

'Why?'

'Because I'm sure that up there is someone who has a connection with Finer Foods and knows about you and her. If we can only identify who that is, we can find the murderer.' Darina thought she knew who it was but without the missing connection she had no proof.

'But the police have already talked to Betty.'

'Maybe they didn't ask her the right questions.' As Jane seemed not so much to hesitate as lack any belief the journey could yield anything useful, Darina added, 'We've got to try, you must see that.'

Slowly, reluctantly, Jane nodded.

Darina let out a long sigh. If Jane had refused, she would have gone anyway but it would have been much more difficult to talk to Mrs Bright.

'When do you want to go?'

'Now.'

Jane stared, then accepted the decision without further question.

Half an hour later they were driving in Darina's car towards Woodbridge in Suffolk.

As they travelled across England, Darina appreciated just how ideal Betty Bright had been for the murderer's purposes. The journey took some four hours and that was driving fast. Nobody would want to turn round after arriving towards the end of the day and drive back again, even if they had suspected something was wrong. The natural thing to do was wonder what had happened and take the opportunity of an evening with an old friend, stay the night, and return next morning. Even starting out as early as Jane had, she would have arrived back too late to save Joel from his diabetic coma.

Chapter Thirty

Betty Bright lived in a modern estate of well-designed small houses within convenient walking distance of the shops.

Jane rang the bell. While they waited Darina looked round at the other houses. Was it her imagination or did a lace curtain flutter across the way?

Then the door was opened by a woman in her early forties with unremarkable looks. She gave Jane a warm embrace. 'What a terrible time you've been having,' she said as she took their coats. 'I was so pleased to get your call, are you going to stay?'

'I can't. There's the shop, you see.'

'You should find someone reliable to look after it for a bit.'

They were led through to a small over-furnished front room in which every available surface was thronged with small ornaments. A loaded tea tray stood ready. 'I'm sure you haven't had anything on that awful journey. I'll just make the tea, you help yourselves to something to eat.'

Darina attacked the sandwiches with grateful alacrity. Jane picked the cucumber out of hers and left the bread.

'Now,' said Betty when tea had been poured, half the sandwiches eaten, and Darina was working her way through a piece of excellent sponge cake. 'What exactly is it I can do to help?'

Darina had been summing their hostess up as she exchanged small talk with her about the town, their trip, and various baking methods.

Betty Bright, she judged, was a self-reliant woman of firm convictions. She knew from Jane that she was a skilled computer programmer who worked from home, that she had returned to this coastal town to live with her mother after leaving her husband. The move to her present house had come after her mother's death a couple of years earlier.

'I expect you know that just before Joel Madoc was arrested

182

for the murder of Marian Drax, Jane was lured up here so that an attempt could be made on his life.'

It seemed the woman hadn't known the complete story. 'Jane just arrived one night thinking I was in some trouble. I told the police who questioned me I hadn't sent her any message, it was as much a puzzle to me as it was to her. But what a shocking thing! What happened?'

Darina gave brief details of the diabetic coma and watched the concern in their hostess's face.

'All right now, is he?' Betty asked Jane. The other woman nodded wordlessly.

'Did the police ask you whether you knew anyone with any connections with Finer Foods?' Darina continued.

'Yes, they did. But as far as I know, there isn't anyone and that's what I told them. I mean, it's not as if I know anything about the firm, apart from what Jane's told me.' She looked at her still silent friend. 'I was so pleased when I heard she'd found someone else. I thought life was about to make something up to her for all she'd had to suffer.'

'You've never married again?'

'No.' The answer was brisk. 'Ken did for me as far as men were concerned.' Betty's lips thinned, her eyes hardened, the unremarkable features suddenly became memorable, formed themselves into the face of a bitter woman who didn't forget. 'I cheered when I heard he was dead; as far as I was concerned Jane deserved a medal and I wrote and told her so. The one good thing Ken ever did was to bring us together.'

'After the trial, I don't think I could have kept going if it hadn't been for Betty,' Jane said. 'I just wanted to curl up and die but she kept at me to change my name and start a new life.'

'Couldn't let Ken win in the end,' Betty said briskly. 'That's what I told her.' She looked at Darina. 'People who didn't know him as Jane and I did couldn't understand. If you had met him, you'd probably have fallen for him, too. He was handsome, fun, full of life. Yes, he liked a drink now and then and perhaps a bit more often than now and then. But you'd believe he'd give all that up once he had a secure home, a woman who loved him.

'Then when he started hitting you, you'd believe it was your fault, it had to be something you'd said or done and you'd promise yourself to be more careful, make sure you didn't do anything that could provoke him again. Because in between times he was everything you could ever want. But eventually you'd begin to realize that things were never going to get better. That the drinking wasn't getting better but worse. That it wasn't your fault he was beating you, it was something he needed to do, it gave him a real kick. I could just about stand it for myself, after all, I'd married him, he was my husband for better for worse, but when he started on Jeremy' – she glanced at a snapshot on the mantelpiece of a youngster in a school blazer and cap – 'that was it. I wasn't going to have my son brought up in a home where he was constantly terrified either his mother or he was going to be beaten to death. So I left and came here.' She paused. 'I was the lucky one.'

'That's exactly how it was with Mike, my husband,' Jane said, appearing animated for the first time that day. 'I should have recognized the signs when I met Ken.' There was self-hate in her voice now. 'He was another destroyer, someone who could hit the way Mike hit me. I'd been standing at the top of the stairs and by the time I reached the bottom, I knew it was all over with the baby. If I'd had the strength I would have killed him. I'd lost everything, my marriage, my self-respect, and now my baby. But when the hospital discharged me, I just walked out, picked up as many pieces of my life as I could, and found myself right back in the same sort of relationship. How can one be so stupid?'

'People talk about the victim syndrome,' Betty said. 'As though a victim seeks his fate, gives off particular vibrations that are picked up by their violators. I don't go along with that but I do think maybe women like Jane and me are attracted to particular men who are looking for something. We think it's love and security but actually they need a woman who won't stand up to them, one they can kick around and abuse any way they can think of.'

Darina saw the look that passed between the two women. It belonged to sisters in arms who had been through fire. The experience had hardened and toughened Betty Bright; had it done the same to Jane? She seemed pliant and gentle, yet she had taken that knife and plunged it into Ken Bright's guts. And had wanted to do the same to her husband. Just what had Joel Madoc taken on?

For the first time Darina asked herself whether Jane Leslie was actually the right woman for the volatile Anglo-Italian. Was she as warm, soft, and caring as she appeared? Would she be able to hold a man with a libido as active as Joel's? Eleanor Drax had known she had to allow him a certain freedom, would Jane need to? Would she be willing to? Then Darina wondered about the capacity of a passionate man for violence. Was it latent in Joel, could it be used, not against Jane but to protect her? Had she, Darina wondered, made another terrible mistake and brought them here on a fool's errand?

She turned to Betty Bright. 'We have to find out if any of your neighbours knew Jane's real identity and if they have a connection with Finer Foods.'

'You really believe there could be someone like that?'

Darina firmly buried any doubts she might have. 'Someone wanted to remove Joel Madoc. The first attempt on his life failed, Marian Drax died instead, and they had to try again. Whoever it is knew about the twin sinks in the kitchen, knew about Joel's diabetes, that Jane was living with him and also that she would respond to a plea from you. It must be someone close to Joel and part of Finer Foods. He's fighting for control there, you know.'

The woman looked doubtful. 'Most of my friends have met Jane on various visits but I never told anyone about her past. Any more than I talk about mine.'

Darina pounced on that. 'Who knows how your ex-husband died?'

Betty looked resigned. 'At the time some local reporter got on to the story, Heaven knows how, and did a short piece on battered wives that linked me in and included the fact that I'd contacted Jane. It was before I moved, though, and I don't think anybody round here would have thought twice about it. For Jeremy's sake as much as mine I keep quiet about Ken, he's been hurt enough by his father.'

Betty might believe none of her near neighbours knew of her past; Darina was convinced, had to be convinced, that one of them did. Who maybe wasn't particularly interested in the details but had a visitor at some time who recognized Jane Leslie. A visitor who was interested enough to enquire about her and dig out the full story about her friend, then had followed it up to discover Jane's secret.

She asked Betty to run through each of her neighbours, listening desperately for some clue that would give her the lead she needed. There seemed nothing until Betty started talking about a widow, Margaret Wilson, who lived in one of the houses opposite hers. Apparently she had recently lost her third husband; her first had also died, her second marriage had ended in divorce, after which she had returned to Woodbridge, her home town, and renewed an old friendship. As Betty was recounting the brief happiness she had found with him, she suddenly paused.

'What is it?' pressed Darina. 'What have you thought of?'

'It may be nothing, really. It was just that we were discussing once the trauma of losing one's mother and Margaret started to tell me about coming back from abroad for the funeral of hers, she hardly lived in England at all with either of her first two husbands, and how difficult it was selling her old family home, when she suddenly changed the subject, the way you do when you think you could embarrass someone. I didn't think much of it at the time but I discovered later that her mother had lived very close to mine. Then I realized that she probably knew about Ken and everything and didn't want me to know that she knew, if you see what I mean. Well, that suited me so I sort of forgot about it. She's a nice woman, much older than me but I like her, we often drop into each other's houses for coffee.'

'Would you call her a bit of a gossip?'

Betty smiled, back to the nice, unremarkable woman she had seemed when they arrived. 'She certainly knows everything about everyone, always has a story about one of the neighbours. Nothing unpleasant, you know, she's just really interested in what's going on. People and cooking are her things, she says.'

'Cooking?'

'Oh, everywhere she's gone in the world, she's collected recipes. She was thrilled to meet Jane and hear about her delicatessen. Do you remember Margaret Wilson, Jane? She came over for coffee while you were here about a year ago.'

Jane nodded with no real interest.

'Does she have any family?' Darina asked, trying to contain a mounting sense of excitement.

Betty hesitated then said, 'I know she's got a son in the Army, at least, he was in the Army but I think he left a little while ago to do something else.'

Darina let out a long sigh. Their journey had paid off, the connection had been found.

Chapter Thirty-One

Betty Bright asked them to stay the night but Darina wanted to return to Somerset as soon as possible and Jane turned down the suggestion that she remain on her own.

'Do you think this really will clear Joel?' she asked on the way back.

Darina was by no means certain, she still had no concrete evidence to produce, only a series of circumstances that, to her, added up to the only possible explanation of all that had happened. But would it produce the same equation for Chief Inspector Melville?

'Every chance,' she said with as much conviction as she could muster.

They drove the next few miles in silence. Then, 'Joel has been trying to see me,' Jane offered.

'I'm sure he has.'

'Perhaps I should at least have a talk with him?'

'Of course you should.' Darina wanted to add something about how they needed each other but she was no longer certain of their future together.

'I'm not a complete fool, you know,' said Jane suddenly. 'I know he's probably incapable of being faithful to one woman. He's that sort of man. But it would be preferable to being beaten. Wouldn't it?'

Darina thought giving her opinion, which was that either choice sounded appalling, would be pointless.

Most of the rest of the journey was completed in silence. Then as they approached Somerset Jane asked, 'Could you possibly take me to Joel's rather than the shop?'

Darina drove up to Joel's astonishing house hardly able to believe it was only a matter of weeks since the evening she had come for supper. As on that occasion, the huge windows spilled light on to the dark garden. Inside, Darina and Jane could see Joel slumped in his chair. A glass stood on the table in front of him. There was no other sign of life.

Jane wrenched open the car door as Darina drew up, stumbled on the gravel then found her way to the front entrance and hammered on the door. Darina, sitting exhausted in her seat, saw the sound slowly penetrate to Joel, saw him get to his feet and come to the door. She closed her eyes. At this point she should drive away but she was too tired. The round journey on top of the remains of the jet lag from her flight back from Hong Kong had taken all her energy. It wasn't even as though William was waiting for her, he was working that evening.

So when Joel opened her car door and told her to come inside, she uncoiled her weary limbs and obeyed.

Once in the house, she could see that he, too, had been changed by the experiences of the last few weeks. He'd lost weight, his loosely hanging clothes looked as though they had been slept in; the planes of his face had turned from being strong to gaunt, their hollows emphasized by the stubble that was a long way from being designer. The brown eyes had all the warmth of the walking dead. Except when he looked at Jane. They sat close together on the leather sofa, holding hands, each seemingly content to be with the other.

Joel had offered alcohol but Darina had asked instead for coffee and this now stood with cheese and biscuits on the low table before them.

Jane made Darina tell the story of their trip.

'So you see,' she said at the end, 'I was right but I have no proof I can present to the police.'

'It makes much more sense than the case they've put together against me,' protested Joel. 'And to think I told Anna today that I would sell her my shares and get out of Finer Foods.'

'You did?' Jane was amazed. 'But I thought you were dedicated to the firm.'

He gave a wry smile. 'It was Eleanor's baby, I wanted to succeed with it in memory of her.' He turned to the woman sitting beside him and gave her a gentle kiss. 'You know she was a loving wife and I shall remember her for the rest of my life. But I never felt for her one half of what I feel for you. When it seemed I'd lost you, nothing else mattered. In jail, waiting for that wretched lawyer to get a move on and organize my bail, I realized what my priorities should be. What the hell was I doing spending my time fighting with Anna, trying to succeed with a company that appeared determined to run itself into the ground? Let her grapple with it if that was what she wanted. Maybe Eleanor was wrong and she has what it takes. I really couldn't care any longer. I had to concentrate on convincing the police I had nothing to do with Marian's death. Even that didn't seem very important if I had lost you.'

Jane said nothing, just moved a little closer to him.

'And what do you feel about Finer Foods now?' Darina asked.

'Now? Now I'm fighting mad. I cannot understand how I never realized just what was going on. And I still can't quite believe that, that . . .' He couldn't bring himself to finish the sentence. 'But I'm damned if I'm going to let Eleanor's company get away from me. We've got a board meeting scheduled for tomorrow afternoon. You've given me the information I need and I shall make good use of it.'

'I'll be telling the police everything tomorrow morning,' Darina said, wondering exactly what Joel's intentions were.

'After you've finished with them, come to the office. I'd like you at the meeting to back up what I'm going to say, and I want Jane there too.'

Energy had been reborn in Joel. There was little trace now of the crushed man Jane had woken with her knocking. Now the dynamism Darina had seen when they first met had re-emerged. She wondered if the police would act on her information, would prevent the meeting going ahead. Half of her hoped they would, the other half wanted to see how Joel handled it.

Darina finished her coffee and managed to gather sufficient energy to get back in her car and complete the journey home, refusing the second offer she had had that day of a bed for the night.

Chapter Thirty-Two

The directors of Finer Foods were gathered round the board-room table when Darina was shown into the room. Joel was sitting in the heavy armchair at the top. Carefully dressed in a pinstripe suit of dark charcoal with a shirt in fine stripes of blue and red and a dark red tie, he looked in command of any situation that might arise. A pristine white handkerchief poked out of the top of his breast pocket and he presented a welcome contrast to the unshaven man of last night.

On his right was Anna Drax Johnson, triumphant in a suit of lime-green wool, her hair rivalling a newly revealed chestnut. Her almond-shaped tiger's eyes were gleaming with excitement, her cheeks were flushed. She couldn't have looked more beautiful on her wedding day. Across the table from her was Michael Berkeley, soberly dressed as usual, his shirt cuffs of pale blue sporting a pair of elaborately worked gold cuff links. His hands quietly fid-dled with a ball-point pen.

Further down the table was Peter Drax, dapper in a light tweed suit, its cut counteracting any bucolic tendency of the material. He looked mystified and impatient, one hand tapping irritably on the table.

Separated a little from the others sat Jane Leslie, her face exhausted but content, her figure dressed in a plain skirt and twin set. Darina looked wryly at her own tweed skirt and thick sweater; the two of them appeared to be the only ones who had given no thought to their outfits.

As she was shown in by Maggie, Peter said, 'Can we please start? I don't know what all this is about but I have to be back in my surgery by five o'clock.'

'Ah, Darina,' said Joel. 'Come and sit here.' He rose and arranged a chair beside Jane for her. 'Now,' he said as he resumed his seat, 'I think we can start.'

'Just a moment.' It was Anna, a ghost of unease crossing her features. 'I don't understand why Jane and Darina are here. This is a Finer Foods board meeting and I object to the presence of outsiders.'

'We can hold our board meeting afterwards, if you still want to, Anna. At the moment I have something to say and I wish Jane and Darina to hear it.'

'Look, I can't stay here for ever. Let's have the board meeting now and you can say whatever you want to after that.'

'Peter, I'll be quite happy for you to leave whenever you feel you have to,' Joel said imperturbably. He looked round the table, his glance challenging, sparkling.

Anna began to look uneasy, Michael stared at his ball-point pen as it slid between his fingers, Peter's eyes narrowed suspiciously.

Darina hoped that Joel was going to have more luck this afternoon than she had had that morning with Chief Inspector Melville.

At the end of her interview, she had felt both foolish and furious. He had listened to her with patience and courtesy, making notes of several points. He had glanced through the folder of information on Patrick Browne, and put it on one side. He had, however, questioned her with particular closeness on everything she had seen in the kitchen after Marian Drax's body had been discovered. Then he had thanked her for coming without betraying any hint of his reactions or if he had changed his mind on Joel Madoc's guilt. When she challenged him to agree with what she had suggested, he produced a small, tight smile and said he was grateful for her information but that it was impossible to say at this stage how important it could prove.

Finally, frustrated but aware that what she had had to offer could hardly be called concrete evidence, Darina could do nothing further but say goodbye and leave. Now, sitting beside Jane, Darina found herself willing Joel to succeed where she felt she had failed. She had hoped the police could step in but it looked as though the Finer Foods mystery would have to be resolved without her help.

Joel fingered his breast-pocket handkerchief, adjusting its set, then began. 'I think you are all aware that this meeting was originally called in order that I could resign from the board and offer my shares for sale.'

'That is exactly what will happen,' Anna said sharply. 'You have no alternative, Joel. You are charged with murder, the company has suffered drastically under your direction, and the shareholders cannot tolerate the situation.'

'Ah, yes, the shareholders. Let us be quite clear what the situation is. I own forty-five per cent of the voting stock. If the rest of you all close ranks, you can, of course, vote me off the board. That has been the position ever since Eleanor died and left me her shares. Now, I know that as managing director I was welcomed with as much warmth as out-of-date fishpaste, so presumably you have been unable to agree amongst yourselves on the appropriate action.

'Anna, my dear stepdaughter, I know exactly where you stand. You hoped to be managing director yourself after your mother died and have been leading the campaign against me.'

The Marketing Director sat in her seat, her expression as glazed as an instantly frozen prawn, her eyes fixed on the table.

Joel turned his attention next to the Sales Director. 'Michael, you also felt you should have been appointed managing director and, though you have, with your ineffable tact, appeared to try and mediate between Anna and myself, I have no doubt at all whose side you would come down on should it come to a vote.'

The gold biro slipped through the fingers a little more quickly but nothing else suggested Michael Berkeley's equilibrium had been disturbed.

'Marian I cannot, of course, ask.' Joel hesitated a moment then added, 'I regret very much the impulse of a moment that made me turn to her for comfort shortly before Eleanor died. I'm afraid she converted what was no more, or less, than the reaching out of a man in torment for some sign there was still some warmth in the world, into a declaration of lasting love. It was painful to have to disillusion her and I can understand if she felt unable to forgive me. Yet, I wonder if she totally gave up hope of my turning to her again? Did she waver sometimes in her support of you, Anna? Refuse to join you in an open board room confrontation?'

Anna's gaze flicked nervously from Joel to the Sales Director, then returned to gazing at the table in front of her.

'Peter, you I know have absolutely no interest whatsoever in the company beyond your dividends. Did you suggest when Anna came to you that it would be a shame to rock the boat, that things were going along very nicely as they were?'

'I couldn't see any sense in what she was suggesting,' Peter said bluntly. 'I'm sorry, Anna,' he said as she turned to him with a sharply indrawn breath. 'I know you asked me never to mention it to Joel but he seems to know all about it anyway. You've always wanted to have everything your own way. As long as Dad was alive, he saw you got it. But Mother was a better judge of character. If she didn't feel you could run the firm, then I was damned if I was going to give you control.'

'You didn't think she was a good judge of character as far as Fiona was concerned.' Anna had a vicious whip to her voice.

'Mother was absolutely right about Fiona,' he said with steady dignity. 'But I happen to love her. And I can forgive those I love,' he added pointedly.

'So,' Joel ignored the flush that blazed on Anna's high cheekbones. 'We have the situation where you can't command enough support to overthrow me. But Marian's feelings of bitterness towards me can be worked on and you know your brother's weakness, he needs the money his company shares bring in. If that income could be reduced, perhaps then he could be induced to consider the Managing Director incompetent and agree to replace him.

'So you conceive the idea of setting up a company in Hong Kong that will be a middle man between Finer Foods and their agent, creaming off part of the profits. No doubt that is now nicely banked waiting for you to gain control of the company. But you couldn't do that on your own, could you? You put it to Marian, as financial director, that it would be a secret way for her to revenge herself on me. Perhaps you suggested that the arrangement would only be for a short time, just long enough to teach me that, whatever my business track record, I didn't know how to run a food company. And you persuaded her. What argument did you use with Michael?'

The Sales Director lifted his head sharply, seemed about to protest.

'Oh yes, Michael, you had to be in it as well. You would never have swallowed the need for another agent and I have enough respect for your abilities to know that you wouldn't have accepted Patrick Browne, ex-soldier, no experience, as a bona fide member of Mr Wu's firm.'

Michael Berkeley compressed his lips and used his ball-point pen to gouge deep lines in the pad resting in front of him.

'But you always need money, don't you Michael, and I am sure a little financial inducement made up your mind quite quickly for you.

'So, Anna, you set up your little company. Quite a test for the new Managing Director. Would he realize what you had done? Unlikely, considering how little he knew of the company's business and the unavailability of any past figures. Would he manage to increase business enough not to make the losses on the Oriental side noticeable? If I did, it would mean I could after all run Finer Foods. Did you tell your fellow conspirators that, if that proved the case, you would give up your campaign? But, as you planned, I failed; the recession wasn't on my side and there were other losses I had no reason to suspect the existence of.'

'I really have no idea what you are talking about,' Anna broke in roughly, her colour high. 'It's true we've got a new agent in Hong Kong but the story you have built around his appointment is a complete farradiddle.'

'Is it? Darina Lisle has been out to Hong Kong and spoken with Mr Wu. If you like, she will tell you exactly what he said.'

'I am afraid I found Mr Wu unreliable and had to safeguard our interests there.'

'Have you been safeguarding them? How is it we have been receiving substandard stock? Stock not bought through Mr Wu?'

'That's what he claims,' Anna spat out angrily.

'I think if we examine the accounts of Far East Foods and of The Far East Food Company, we'll find the truth of the matter. I am, of course, assuming that Mr Browne has been keeping accounts of some sort. But I am sure he realizes some reckoning has to be made at the end of the day.

'Let us consider that, for a moment. The end of the day. Did it seem too long coming? Was Marian getting restless, worried, with my pressing to have the accounts put into better order? Did it look as though the plan might be discovered before you managed to get rid of me? Is that why you decided I had to go in a rather more permanent way?'

Peter Drax had been listening to Joel with cool attention. Now he said quietly, 'Are you suggesting my sister has been trying to murder you? That Aunt Marian's death was a mistake?'

'Exactly. Marian was the unfortunate victim of a break in the power supply and I was its benefactor.'

'But Anna couldn't have had anything to do with it, she was nowhere near the office that morning.'

'Any more than Michael or you were. It was a very clever plan. The drawback was that in order to have a water-tight alibi, an unfortunate phrase perhaps considering what happened, the

194

murderer could not be on hand to take action when the power unexpectedly failed.'

Darina could see that Anna was no longer flushed, she was paler than the paper pads on the board-room table.

'The sinks were wired up the night before with an automatic timer set to switch on the current to them some time after I started my session in the kitchen. Unfortunately, the power failure stopped the clock and the delay meant the current to the sink wasn't activated until after I had finished my washing up and, all unknowingly, left the sinks live for poor Marian.'

'But no automatic timer was found,' said Michael Berkeley steadily, his gaze fixed on Anna.

'No,' said Joel. 'That is where Darina comes in again.' He turned to where she was sitting with Jane Leslie.

'I'm afraid,' she said clearly, 'I took too much for granted. I told the police that all Patrick Browne did when we entered the kitchen together was turn off the tap and take out some towels from the cupboard to mop up the water. I assumed that a bystander was no more than that and it never occurred to me that he could have pocketed a timer from the power outlet at the back of the sink cupboard without my noticing while I was examining Marian Drax's body. It was a very serious error and could have meant that the murderer was free to make a second attempt to kill Joel.'

'But it's thanks to the prompt and intelligent action of you and your fiancé that I'm alive today. The police believed that my diabetic coma was self-induced, to divert suspicion, make everyone believe what was in fact the truth, that someone was trying to kill me. You all knew about my diabetes and that I kept insulin in my office fridge. You all had access to that office. Peter, you were in there the day before I collapsed.'

The doctor threw down his pencil. 'You're not suggesting that *I* tried to murder you?' His indignation was almost too extreme. 'I never heard anything so monstrous.'

'You are beginning, my dear Joel,' said Anna, 'to sound just like M. Poirot. You can't know what you are talking about.' Her manner was studiedly calm but Darina noticed that her hands were clasped tightly together as though to stop any tendency to shake. 'All right' – the Marketing Director started to speak more quickly, her words running together in their eagerness to be heard – 'I admit the Hong Kong company was set up more or less as you

195

suggested. The money is all there, none of it has been touched. It was, as you said, a way of getting you out of the company. It wasn't right of Mother to bring you in, it wasn't fair. But I never suggested murder. I would never have anything to do with that, never.'

There might have been the slightest softening in Joel's face as he looked at her. 'No,' he said, 'I don't believe you would. On the other hand,' he turned to Michael, 'you would and did.'

Chapter Thirty-Three

The Sales Director's gold biro bit deeply into his pad. Then he stopped doodling and laid the pen carefully on the table. 'You will have to work hard to pin this on me,' he declared quietly.

'Oh, I think most of the work has been done,' Joel said. 'Despite the mess the accounts were in, we are a fair way towards proving that you have been pocketing part of the restaurant receipts for many years and became greedier after Eleanor's death. Only recently they weren't enough for you. You must have been hard pressed by gambling and other debts, your life style has always been suspiciously affluent; Anna's plan was proving too long drawn out and you couldn't trust Marian's inefficient accounting systems to cover your tracks for very much longer now that a managing director battling with terminal illness had been replaced by one with keener financial instincts.

'Anna,' Joel turned to his stepdaughter, 'I wouldn't be too sure about all the money still sitting in Hong Kong. We shall probably find that part of it at least has either been drawn out or never paid in by Patrick Browne. But we don't have to look far to find out where it has gone. Didn't you wonder just how Michael was able to produce so convenient an agent for you?'

Anna drew a sharp breath. 'Michael?' It was a plea rather than a question.

He sat motionless in his seat, his eyes refusing to meet hers.

She turned to Joel. 'Michael told us he'd heard through a chum that Patrick had just left the Army, knew a lot about food and would be ideal for the company.' She was making no attempt now to pretend that the Hong Kong arrangement had been bona fide.

Joel looked across at Darina.

'Michael and Patrick Browne are half-brothers,' she said and caught a malevolent glance from the Sales Director.

'Half-brothers?' Anna sounded incredulous. 'I never knew

197

Michael had a brother. I can't believe it, surely he would have told us?'

'Michael didn't get on with his stepfather. As soon as he was old enough to leave home, he severed contact with his mother, she spent most of her time abroad with her second husband and their child, Patrick, considerably younger than Michael. A few years ago his mother was divorced, came home, and was reunited with her elder son. Michael heard about Patrick leaving the Army from her. He also saw Jane Leslie visiting a house across the road from his mother's and asked what she knew about both her and the woman she was visiting.'

'Michael likes to know odd little facts about the people he works with, don't you, Michael?' interjected Peter Drax. 'Regular old gossip you are when you're in your cups.'

The Sales Director flinched but still said nothing.

'His mother is interested in people as well, she never forgets a detail about them or their lives. So she was able to tell her son all about Betty Bright, who took the extraordinary step of writing to congratulate the killer of her ex-husband. Whether your mother had decided Jane could be the killer or whether you, Michael, researched the case until you found a photograph that confirmed it, I don't know. Did your mother hint and you take it on from there? Whatever, you realized it was the sort of information that could come in very useful in one way or another. You told Marian, didn't you? Was it a way of diverting her from taxing you over the restaurant accounts? Or did you want her to drop the bombshell that Finer Foods' new managing director was involved with someone who had been convicted for manslaughter? That way you wouldn't be involved in the fallout. Unfortunately for you, Marian didn't do more than hint at the truth before she died.

'Then, when you wanted to get Jane out of the way so there would be no one to rescue Joel when he went into a diabetic coma, you remembered your gossipy mother telling you what a good friend she had in Betty Bright.' Darina paused and looked at Michael Berkeley. 'I know how gossipy your mother is, I met her yesterday.' His head jerked at that and his eyes widened. 'She was very pleased to hear I knew you and had met Patrick, did you know I had a long chat with him in Hong Kong?'

His tongue moistened his lips, the pink tip visible for just a minute. There was nothing else to suggest he might lose control.

Darina removed a couple of papers from her bag and laid them on the table in front of her. 'When I got back from seeing your mother last night, I sent a fax to your brother.' She unfolded one of the sheets and read, ' "The automatic timer has been found, think you should fly here immediately, we need to discuss strategy. I saw Mother a few days ago, she's in fine form. Please fax your flight details to this number, security reasons. Also suggest we avoid the telephone.' And I signed it with your name. When I got back home after talking to Chief Inspector Melville this morning, I found an answer. Do you want to see it?'

She held out a small roll of thin paper. Michael Berkeley looked at it as though it were poisoned. Then he slowly held out his hand. He gave the message a quick glance then disdainfully flipped the paper on the table. 'It means nothing, anybody could have sent it, you could have.'

'Have you checked the fax number at the top? That proves it's from Hong Kong.'

Peter Drax picked up the fax as it glided down the table towards him. ' "Nonsense about automatic timer, it was destroyed," ' he read out. 'And then there's a flight number and tomorrow's date.'

'All we have to do is meet the flight,' said Joel matter of factly. 'I suppose it was quite convenient for you that when you failed to kill me with your electrified sink, you got poor Marian instead; you were then in a position to claim any shortfall discovered in the accounts was due to her incompetence.'

Michael's head whipped round and his lips drew back, baring his teeth like a snarling animal. 'Don't ever suggest such a thing,' he grated. 'Marian meant more to me than anyone. It was for her I needed the money. When I found that she had been killed instead of you, it was the most terrible moment of my life. I couldn't let you live after that.' There was a moment when he realized what he had said, his eyelids flickered, their glance sliding sideways, like a cornered creature seeking for an escape route. Then he took a deep breath. 'I didn't mean that the way it sounded.'

There was total silence round the board-room table. Joel had a look of immense satisfaction, Anna appeared stunned, and Peter Drax was checking his watch. Then the telephone rang and Joel picked it up. 'What excellent timing,' he said briskly. 'Tell them to come in, Maggie.'

A moment later the board room door opened and Chief Inspector Melville and another policeman were there. 'Michael Berkeley,' he said, 'I have a warrant for your arrest.'

Darina got home in the early evening to find William in jeans and a sweat shirt investigating the fridge. He was humming happily to himself.

'Why, light of my life, you've come home to me once again, is it to stay this time?' He swept her into his arms for a most satisfactory kiss.

'You're in a rare good humour.' Darina rescued her shopping bag with the steak she had bought on the way home from being crushed between them. 'Have you cracked your case?'

'It's in tiny pieces, walloped with a sledgehammer, we caught the lot last night; like the Mexicans, I could dance on my hat.' He executed a couple of steps. Then took a bottle of sparkling wine from the fridge. 'Tonight we celebrate and tomorrow the team starts the boring business of wrapping up all the evidence, making sure we can make everything stick.' He released the cork from the bottle, poured out two glasses, and handed one to Darina. 'How about you?'

She raised her glass to him. 'I imagine Chief Inspector Melville is saying the same thing back at his station.'

'You never did it?'

'Certainly did. But you tell me about yours first. Sit there and entertain me while I get the meal ready. Guess what, we are having Chinese tonight, a dish your sister's housekeeper taught me after I found out she could do more than shepherd's pie. Except do you want to hang around while I cook rice or shall we have it with noodles?

Noodles were voted for and, as William told her exactly how he and his team had brought to justice a group of house breakers who had been stealing large quantities of property in his area, Darina shredded the steak into small slivers, blanched broccoli, browned almonds, and mixed an oyster-flavoured sauce.

'There,' she said after congratulating him as he came to the triumphant conclusion of his account. 'It's all ready to cook. Will you lay the table, or shall I?'

'I, my lady. You have another glass of wine and tell me the saga of your triumph. You were, if I remember correctly, off to see the Chief Inspector this morning. I looked for a note when I got back a few hours ago but then realized I would have to wait for a progress report until you returned so had a rest instead. Then showered so I would be flower-fresh for you.'

Darina felt it was as well her euphoria matched his.

She gave him a condensed account of her day, ending with the arrival of Chief Inspector Melville. 'He wanted brief statements from us all on the meeting, then Joel produced one of those tiny tape-recorders from his breast pocket and said he would find a verbatim account on that. After which we were all allowed to go home. All, that is, except Michael Berkeley. He was taken off to the station.'

She went over to the hob and put her wok on to heat. 'I was staggered at Melville's arrival, I thought he was still convinced Joel was the murderer and wasn't going to do anything about my information.'

'A chap who plays his cards close to his chest,' murmured William.

'Instead he must have leapt into action the moment I left. They found wire in Michael's garage that matched the cable under the sink and a stack of gambling demands in his desk that amounted to an incredible sum. Apparently his wife was in a dreadful state about the search. She phoned the office but Michael was already in the board room and Maggie said she couldn't put her through, Joel had threatened her with instant dismissal if she disturbed the meeting. It was only when Melville threatened her with equally instant arrest that she was finally persuaded to phone through his arrival.'

'So your epicure is now well and truly in command?'

Darina finished her stir frying, added the sauce, cooked and mixed it in with the beef, placed that in the centre of steam-heated broccoli florets, scattered over the browned almonds, and brought the dish to the table.

'Yes. I don't think he'll have any more trouble with Anna. Whether she will stay or not is another question but he isn't going to prosecute her over the Hong Kong business.'

'And Patrick Browne, what's happening over him? I take it that fax was a mere diversion of your own? Sheer invention?'

Darina nodded. 'I rang Heather and she organized it. Well, it seemed worth a try. And I think it did shake Michael, whatever he claimed, so that Joel's jibe about Marian's death was the final limit. Apparently Michael worshipped her and there was a time she responded. But, Anna said, she didn't want to be the cause of his marriage breaking up and he felt he needed a lot more money before he could afford a divorce. He claimed that was why he went gambling but he must have been born with the instinct, so many of his actions have been those of a gambler. Patrick seems much the same.'

'But didn't Marian have money of her own?'

Darina nodded. 'I think it was one of those convenient arrangements that gave a lot of excitement without needing to stand up to uncomfortable things like divorce and actually living together. Not to mention the fact that she fell in love with Joel.

'Patrick Browne is being taken care of by the Hong Kong police, they are liaising with Melville.' Darina watched William help himself to more of the stir-fry dish then said, 'It will be a long time before I stop feeling a complete idiot over the way it never even occurred to me he might be doing anything under the sink except try to clear up the water. As it was he must have whipped out the timer from the power socket, slipped it into his trench coat pocket, and then reinserted the washing-machine plug. All under my very eyes and without leaving his fingerprints.'

'If I remember your original account, you were examining Marian Drax's body at the time?'

'And should have realized I couldn't take in everything else that was going on,' insisted Darina. 'By the time I looked at him again, his actions seemed totally innocent, a mopping-up operation. But the real mopping-up job had already been done.'

William reached across the table and grasped one of her hands. 'What witnesses will testify they saw with their own eyes can be the bane of any case. They'll swear the mugger wore a blue anorak and actually it was maroon.'

'I'm not sure that makes me feel much better,' said Darina. 'But I hope Chief Inspector Melville also feels ever so slightly foolish over his certainty that Joel was the murderer. You know,' she added reflectively, 'one thing that puzzles me slightly is why Patrick Browne didn't just rip out the whole wiring system, it would have made it an even worse puzzle.'

'Probably he and Berkeley decided that removing all the wires would look too suspicious. After other possibilities, faulty kettles, ovens, etc., had been dismissed, the police would have found the holes in the back of the washing-up machine where the wires were attached to the positive and negative terminals and then their attention would have been focused on who could have removed the cables, which would have put the spotlight squarely on Browne.'

'Being faced with the wrong body must have been a terrible shock, no wonder he appeared a bit punch drunk.'

'Even Michael's second failure to kill Joel nearly achieved its end of getting rid of him as managing director,' commented William. 'Without you he would still be under arrest and Anna would be in control of the company.'

'The whole story is one of a series of failures, in fact.'

'That came out all right in the end.'

'Except for poor Marian Drax.'

Darina made coffee. As she placed it on the table, William asked, 'What of Jane Leslie?'

'She's thinking of putting her delicatessen up for sale and working with Joel. Even if Anna decides to stay, he's going to need a new sales director as well as an accountant.'

'Sounds as though he's got his hands full.'

'Now that he's got a death out of the way, he can get on with running the firm without interference. I think, though, he's put the idea of a chain of delicatessens on one side, at least for the moment. But the book's to go ahead.'

'Great!' Then William hesitated. 'You will have time to get it finished before our wedding, you don't want to postpone it again?'

Darina shook her head. 'As soon as Heather and family are back in England, I'll be walking up the aisle, you're not going to be allowed another extension on your bachelor days.' Then she broke into laughter.

'And what's so funny about my bachelor days?'

'Oh dear.' She wiped her eyes. 'It's nothing to do with that, just that I'm sure your mother meant her kind gift of a trip to Hong Kong to deflect me from being so serious about work and what happened?'

'You used it to further your investigation of murder!' William threw back his head and joined her laughter.

'If I hadn't met up with Patrick Browne and he hadn't described his mother in a way that reminded me of Michael Berkeley's description of his, I might never have made the connection between them. But we won't tell your mother, we'll have both your parents down for a weekend, and I'll just tell them how I got on with your sisters and hand over their presents.

'One thing, though,' she added with decision, 'this is the last time I get involved with murder, I really am useless as a detective.'

William looked at her but said nothing.

JANET LAURENCE
RECIPE FOR
D E A T H

A DELICIOUS CONCOCTION OF CRIME
——————— AND CUISINE ———————

Parted from William Pigram, her detective boyfriend,
Darina Lisle decides to concentrate on her career and
the cookery book she is writing. Little does she realise
she is about to become embroiled in murder... Helping
to judge a cookery contest at a top London hotel, she is
flattered by the attentions of Somerset restaurateur
Simon Chapman, and intrigued to find that Constance
Fry, mother of the winner, runs an organic farm in the
West Country. An invitation to visit is irresistible.

But there are unexplained hostilities between the Fry
family members: Simon Chapman is somehow
involved and so is one of England's greatest cookery
writers. And when tragedy strikes, Darina finds she
must delve deep into the Frys' past in order to unravel
a recipe for death.

JANET LAURENCE
A DEEPE COFFYN

A DELICIOUS CONCOCTION OF CRIME
—————— AND CUISINE ——————

The Society of Historical Gastronomes is
gathering for a weekend symposium on food
from the past. Darina Lisle has been asked to
cater for the occasion and has prepared a
multitude of exquisite dishes – from
salmagundis to a deepe coffyn – culled from
ancient recipe books.

But when the chairman is found stabbed to
death with a boning knife, the professional
pique of the attendant foodies takes on a more
sinister meaning. Discarded lovers, jealous
colleagues and a plagiarised author have
good reason to resent the victim's success.
Darina, too, is under suspicion and
determines to clear her name by revealing the
murderer's true identity.

'Darina's debut performance is immediately
appealing; she should return soon'
Financial Times

Don t miss Janet Laurence's A TASTY WAY
TO DIE and HOTEL MORGUE, featuring
Darina Lisle and available from Headline:
'Filled with mouth-watering recipes as well as
mystery' *Sunday Express*

FICTION/CRIME   0 7472 3772 7

A selection of bestsellers from Headline

All Headline books are available at your local bookshop or newsagent, or can be ordered direct from the publisher. Just tick the titles you want and fill in the form below. Prices and availability subject to change without notice.

Headline Book Publishing PLC, Cash Sales Department, Bookpoint, 39 Milton Park, Abingdon, OXON, OX14 4TD, UK. If you have a credit card you may order by telephone — 0235 831700.

Please enclose a cheque or postal order made payable to Bookpoint Ltd to the value of the cover price and allow the following for postage and packing:
UK & BFPO: £1.00 for the first book, 50p for the second book and 30p for each additional book ordered up to a maximum charge of £3.00.
OVERSEAS & EIRE: £2.00 for the first book, £1.00 for the second book and 50p for each additional book.

Name ....

Address ....

....

....

If you would prefer to pay by credit card, please complete:
Please debit my Visa/Access/Diner's Card/American Express (delete as applicable) card no:

Signature ....Expiry Date ....